Catalans and Others:
History, Culture & Politics in Catalonia, Valencia and the Balearic Islands

John Payne

In respectful memory of

Joan Fuster
(1922–1992)
and
Manuel Vázquez Montalbán
(1939–2003)

Catalans and Others:
History, Culture & Politics in Catalonia, Valencia and the Balearic Islands

John Payne

Five Leaves Publications
www.fiveleaves.co.uk

Catalans and Others
by John Payne

Published in 2016 by Five Leaves,
14a Long Row, Nottingham NG1 2DH

www.fiveleaves.co.uk
www.fiveleavesbookshop.co.uk

ISBN 978-1-910170-24-3

Cover image courtesy of Gill Harry

Typeset and designed by
Four Sheets Design and Print

Printed in Great Britain

Contents

Introduction   9

1. Greater Catalonia?

1. **Factors suggesting unity**   15
    National identities — Spain and regional autonomy
    — Aragon, a shared medieval empire — Jewish and
    Muslim influences — Limitations of *convivència* —
    Incorporation into Spain — Joan Fuster's writings on
    Valencia — Common opposition to Franco regime

2. **Factors suggesting divergence**   25
    Extent of Muslim influence in Valencia — Industrial
    development of Catalonia — Importance of agriculture
    in Valencia — Nineteenth century cultural revival —
    Anti-Catalan and pro-Spanish sentiment in Valencia
    and Balearics — The Catalan Generalitat — North
    Catalonia

3. **A future for Greater Catalonia?**   35
    The parameters of current debate

2. The Mediterranean

1. **The Mediterranean in history**   41
    Links in pre-history — Talayotic culture of Menorca
    and Mallorca — Ibiza and the goddess Tanit —
    Pre-history on the mainland — Greeks and Romans —
    Continuities

2. **The Mediterranean and the modern world**   49
    Catalan visual arts c.1900 — Mir and Rusiñol on
    Mallorca — Joaquín Sorrolla in Valencia — Dalí and
    Picasso

3. **Tourism. The Mediterranean look north**   57
    Spanish isolation after Civil War — Development of
    tourism — John Anthony West, *Osbourne's Army* —
    Impact of tourism

3. Population Movement

1. **A preamble**   65

2. **The three cultures**   65
Christianity — Américo Castro, *The structure of Spanish History* — Impact of Muslims and Jews — Expulsion of Jews — Forced conversion of Muslims — Significance of El Cid — Moriscos — Ramon Llull — Mallorcan Jews and *Xuetes*

3. *Convivència* **and the realities of power**   78

4. **Aragonese and Spanish empires**   80
Catalonia and Aragon — Barcelona, Valencia and Palma as international trade centres — Nineteenth century trade between Catalonia and America

5. **Population movement in the twentieth and twenty-first centuries**   86
Migration within Spain — Migration and tourism — Migration from outside Spain

4. Turbulent Times: Revolting People

1. **A history of revolt 1400–1715**   91
Fifteenth century civil war in Catalonia — The *Germanies* in Valencia and Mallorca c.1520 — War between Catalonia and Spain 1640–59 — War of the Spanish Succession — Loss of local rights in Catalonia and Aragon — Siege of Barcelona 1715 — National days in Catalonia and Valencia

2. **The grace of democracy, 1976–**   102
Catalan autonomous government — Jordi Pujol — Pasqual Maragall — Revised *Estatut* — Rise of the citizens' movements — Òmnium Cultural — Catalan National Assembly — 11 September demonstrations — the 2014 'illegal' referendum — Events in Valencian Community — Reaction in North Catalonia — Uncertain future

5. Silence and Memory   115

The secrets of Franco's Spain — Fuster's *Dictionary for the Idle* — Poetry of Salvador Espriu — Remembering the Civil War — Jorge Semprún and Alain Resnais — Espriu on Spain (*La Pell de Brau*) — Civil War in the Balearic Islands — Post-war reprisals — Remembering the Republic — Bombing of civilians during Civil War — Walter Benjamin at Portbou — Execution of Lluís Companys (1940) — Law of Historical Memory (2007) — Rehabilitation of Josep Renau — Films and historical memory

6. Mind your Language

1. **The development and use of Catalan**   139
Forms of Latin — Development of Catalan — Uneven history of Catalan — Catalan and its dialects — DCVB dictionary — Language policy in Catalonia — Catalan in education — Catalan and Castilian — Linguistic complexity in novels and films

2. **A multilingual musical interlude**   151

3. **Varieties of Catalan**   153
Catalan in North Catalonia — Catalan in Valencia and Balearic Islands — the Wert Law (2014) — Press and media

4. **The current status of Catalan**   158
Why Catalan matters — Catalan as a 'big' language — Language, culture and politics — Global and local

7. Culture, Popular Culture and Everyday Life

1. **The cultures of Greater Catalonia**   163
Varieties of culture — Bidding wars of 'high' culture in Valencia, Castellon and Barcelona — Popular Culture — Cycle of the seasons

2. **Popular culture on the Balearic Islands**   173
Ibiza — Mallorca — Menorca

3. **The Valencian Community celebrates**   176
    'Moors and Christians' festivals — The *Tomatina* in
    Buñol — The Mystery of Elche — The Valencian
    Falles

4. **Popular culture in Catalonia**   181
    Festa Major — Excusionisme — The *sardana* —
    Castellers — Carnaval

5. **Popular culture as community, business and** 184
    politics

8. Catalans and Others

1. The tangled web of globalisation   187

2. The problem of corruption   194

3. 2015: a year of elections   198

4. Greater Catalonia — where is the political   204
    project?

5. Spain and Catalonia: government and   208
    civil society

Introduction
The Catalan-speaking lands

All nationalisms are precisely that: the expression of grievances and claims for the restoration of rights.
Joan Fuster

I have used the term 'Catalan-speaking lands', or Greater Catalonia, to make clear the close linguistic, cultural and historical ties between these areas. No political intent should be inferred. The reasons for making this disclaimer will become apparent as the reader delves into the book.

The Catalan-speaking lands cluster at the western end of the Mediterranean Sea. This book deals with Catalonia, Valencia, the Balearic Islands, and Northern Catalonia in France. The tourist resort and tax haven of Andorra, the Catalan-speaking border area of Aragon (La Franja) and the town of l'Alguer (Alghero in Italian) on Sardinia both lie outside the modest scope of this book.

I have tried to present the distinctiveness of each area, while emphasising the common links of history and culture which bind them. Some would like those links to be stronger. My purpose is not to take a view on this, but to attempt to understand the strong and often antagonistic views of the people who are fortunate enough to inhabit these beautiful lands, all of which are major tourist destinations.

The Balearic Islands are Mallorca, Menorca, Ibiza (Eivissa in Catalan) and Formentera. Together they make up an autonomous region of the Spanish state. The total population is just over one million, of whom 400,000 live in Palma de Mallorca. The dialects of Catalan spoken by the islanders are often referred to as Mallorquí, Menorquí and Eivissenc.

Catalonia (Catalunya) is an autonomous region stretching from the Pyrenees to the Mediterranean as far south as the River Ebro and a little beyond. It is currently engaged in a furious debate both internally and with the Spanish government in Madrid over its possible future independence. It is divided into 41 *comarques* (singular *comarca*) each with strong historical roots. In addition, it is subdivided according to the provinces of the Spanish state, each named after its capital city — Barcelona, Gerona (Girona), Lerida (Lleida) and Tarragona. The largest city by far is Barcelona, which together with its satellite towns is a major industrial and commercial centre

Northern Catalonia (Catalunya Nord) consists of five *comarques* ceded to France by the Treaty of the Pyrenees in 1714. Roussillon (Rosselló) includes the important city of Perpignan (Perpinyà) but the whole area stretches up into the Pyrenees nearly as far as Andorra. Because of the centralised nature of France, Northern Catalonia is not recognised for administrative purposes, but is included in the region of Languedoc-Roussillon.

Valencia is a third autonomous region within Spain stretching from just south of the Ebro to Murcia. It includes the Spanish provinces of Castellon (Castelló de la Plana), Valencia, and Alicante (Alacant). Inland it extends into mountainous terrain separating it from Aragon and Castile. The local language is usually referred to as Valencià. Hostility towards Catalonia is a significant political force, and usually includes the claim that Valencian is a separate language rather than a dialect of Catalan. While both Alicante and Valencia City are industrial and commercial centres and ports, agriculture, especially rice and fruit growing, remains a significant part of the economy.

* * * * * *

The present moment in Greater Catalonia is one of flux. The current revival of separatist sentiment in the Autonomous Region of Catalonia raises new questions about the sense Catalan people have of their own past, its distinctiveness, its future, and its relationship with the other Catalan-speaking territories.

Broadening the focus of my previous books about Catalonia to include French Catalonia, the Balearic Islands and Valencia foregrounds important questions about why territories with a long, shared past choose to understand their present in such diverse ways. And why there is fierce debate within those territories about issues of language, culture, identity and history.

First of all, a word about the dedication of this book. Manuel Vázquez Montalbán was a Barcelona writer. One of his early Pepe Carvalho detective novels, available in English, was *Los Mares del Sur* (*Southern Seas*). It is about the dream of evasion, escape from the humdrum and everyday, which for so many English lies at the heart of our love of the Mediterranean in general and for the Mediterranean shores of Spain and the Balearic Islands in particular.

Joan Fuster has provided the epigrams which punctuate my own text, all except one taken from his great work *Diccionari per a ociosos* (1964, available in English as *Dictionary for the Idle*). The word great is no rhetorical exaggeration: Fuster's book celebrates human and creative freedom, yet was written and published under the military dictatorship of General Francisco Franco, a regime which denied all the values for which Fuster stood. Thanks to Ross Bradshaw at Five Leaves and the Anglo-Catalan Society, this masterpiece is now available in English.

11

It may come as some sort of surprise to an English reader to know that both men were notorious in their own back-yards. Vázquez Montalbán because of his Communism and his use of the Castilian rather than Catalan language. Fuster because of his commitment to the concept of Greater Catalonia — a term I have borrowed to represent the concept of *Els Països Catalans*, the Catalan lands, the shared homeland of those who speak Catalan, Valencian, and the three Balearic dialects. Fuster survived an assassination attempt in 1981 when his house was bombed by right-wing extremists. He has been vigorously criticised by those who reject a Catalan dimension to their Valencian identity, as well as by others who are quite happy to think of themselves as 'Spanish'.

If this book has a single purpose, it is perhaps to explain how such subtleties of language, culture and history can give rise to such passions. I have tried very hard not to take sides, a difficult if not impossible task, and I hope the reader will appreciate my attempts to understand and evaluate rather than adulate or condemn.

I think it will help the reader as s/he goes through the book to bear in mind four words which those in any of the places under consideration might use to describe themselves and their homeland:

La gent — the people (population)
El poble — the people (national identity)
La nació — the nation (political)
El país — the country (area)

Potentially, they are all dangerous words, especially *poble* and *nació*. As we have seen in recent European history they can excite both love and hatred, inspire commitment and a sense of social inclusiveness, but also rapidly decay into xenophobia and violence.

With regard to place-names, I have used what I consider to be the most recognisable forms to an English language reader. The most important ones are listed in the table at the end of the book. For other places for which there is a commonly used English form, I have tended to use that first with Catalan in brackets when the name first occurs in the text, e.g. Collioure (Cotlliure).

Finally, I would like to acknowledge the help, advice and friendship, in some cases spanning a period of twenty-five years, of all those people who have eased my path as a writer about the Catalan lands and peoples. I would not expect them to agree with the views I have put forward but I hope they will respect my sincerity and my commitment.

Chapter 1
Greater Catalonia?

Most foreigners' judgement of us is that we are horrible. With such an attitude they themselves confirm our sense of difference ... According to them, we are a jealous, pagan lot, inclined to mirthful obscenity, rationalistic, miserly, garrulous, easygoing, licentious and litigious, split up into tiny and irreconcilable tribes. All of this is true. The only thing is that we don't quite appreciate why such characterisations are necessarily to be taken as criticisms.

Factors suggesting unity

For many of the inhabitants of Spain, national identity is not an issue. It is as if Spain has always existed, will always exist, a sovereign state, a member of the European Union, the United Nations and countless other international bodies. When Spain's democratic constitution was negotiated in the late 1970s, following the death of General Franco, the anxieties of Catalans and Basques in particular about their own national identities were 'solved' by the application of a wholesale system of autonomous regions.

Although some of these areas, including Catalonia and the Basque Country, have rather more powers than others, it remains a Spanish national system. Thus an autonomous region such as La Rioja, the main common interest of which is in the protection of its valuable wine *denominación de origen*, has the same legal basis as the Valencian Community, the Balearic Islands or Catalonia, with their many centuries of separate history and institutions, their own language and cultural traditions. In that sense regional autonomy as defined by the Spanish constitution is of limited value to those Basques and Catalans who identify themselves as 'a nation'.

The unity of Spain is explicitly stated in the constitution. If it had not been, it is unlikely that the army, a powerful force in Spain even after the death of Franco, would have agreed to a constitution which turned Spain from a military dictatorship into a democratic state. Further, it states that under no circumstances can autonomous regions join with one another. In other words, both the political projects of an independent Catalonia or of a united Greater Catalonia are unconstitutional.

In this chapter, it is my intention to explore some of the factors that suggest not just strong links but indeed a potential unity between the lands of Greater Catalonia, as defined in my Introduction. Firstly there is the shared medieval empire. Not the 'Catalan' empire because it was always ruled in the name of the Kingdom of Aragon, based in Castilian-speaking Saragossa. Thus although the economic power-house was Catalonia (and in particular its major sea-port, Barcelona) the kings ruled as monarchs of Aragon, Catalonia and Valencia, with each kingdom having its own fiercely defended rights and representative institutions. For a time in the thirteenth and fourteenth century a separate kingdom linked the Catalan-speaking area of Roussillon in modern France with Mallorca, which explains the splendid Gothic palace in Perpignan called the 'Palace of the Kings of Mallorca'. From 1344 King of Mallorca (including the smaller islands of Menorca, Ibiza and Formentera) became another title of the Aragonese kings.

Catalan was the common language of the empire, which at various times extended over much of the Mediterranean, with consulates in the Middle East, Turkey, Greece and North Africa. As we shall explore further in chapter 4, it was an empire characterised by violence as well as more civilised standards. When Menorca was conquered from the Muslims in 1287, there was extensive 'ethnic cleansing': those who could escaped by sea, and those who stayed were slaughtered and replaced by Catalan settlers from the mainland. This process had previously been executed with greater or lesser degrees of bloodshed on Ibiza and Mallorca, and reached its most brutal climax at Alghero (l'Alguer) in Sardinia. Cultural nationalists who point with pride to the persistence of a dialect of Catalan in this small Sardinian town do well to also recall the sordid beginnings of this colony. Ramon Muntaner, the author of an amusing, if often violent, chronicle of the Catalan soldiers-of-fortune who spent considerable periods in both Turkey and Greece, can offer no greater praise of a town than that its inhabitants speak the 'most beautiful Catalan in the world'. He rather spoils it by awarding this rather exclusive accolade to rather a lot of places.

Life in the Aragonese Empire became more complicated when Ferdinand of Aragon married Isabella of Castile in 1469, thus uniting the two major political powers of the Iberian Peninsula. Isabella of Castile, encouraged by the religious orders, especially the Dominicans, wanted to end once and for all the existence of Jewish communities in her lands. With the two crowns now united, there was pressure on Aragon to implement a common policy on Jews, despite the reluctance of Ferdinand. There were thriving Jewish communities not just in the big cities — Barcelona, Valencia, Palma de Mallorca, but also in relatively small towns, such as Besalú, Tortosa and Gerona in Catalonia. Indeed, Gerona was an important centre of Jewish life and scholarship that attracted students from across Europe, with a substantial ghetto (the *call*) located near the cathedral and the main street of the old town, the Carrer de la Força (once the Roman Via Augusta). Under both Muslim rule and Christian rule, one-in-ten of the urban population of the Aragonese lands was a Jew.

While Jews made valuable contributions to both economic and administrative life in medieval Aragon,

Christian kings proved less adept at protecting their Jewish populations than Muslim rulers. Successive pogroms from the thirteenth to the fifteenth centuries had already reduced substantially the Jewish population by the time of Ferdinand's accession to the throne of Aragon. The expulsion of the Jews from Spain in 1492, reluctantly agreed to by Ferdinand, was a tragedy in cultural terms, but the truth was that most of the Jewish *aljamas* (communities) were already much reduced in size. The Sephardic diaspora was a long, lingering death rather than a sudden cataclysmic event.

The other disaster of 1492 for the Aragonese lands occurred far away across the Atlantic Ocean. It was the arrival of Christopher Columbus in America. The enormous statue on a column which dominates the port of Barcelona points eastwards, ironically, towards the lands of the medieval Aragonese Empire. But Columbus' voyages marked the new orientation of Spain westwards towards the New World and America. There were complaints and revolts, as we shall see, but for the next few centuries, the Mediterranean lands became a backwater of the project of Greater Spain. It included for a while Portugal (1580–1640) but also increasingly involvement through the Hapsburg Kings and Emperors with the wider European scene, especially the Low Countries (now Belgium and the Netherlands) and the Central European Hapsburg Empire. Spanish gold financed imperial Hapsburg ambitions rather than the development of agriculture and industry in Iberia.

The impact of this reorientation of the Spanish world away from the Mediterranean and towards America and Europe was not helped by policy towards Jews and Muslims. In general terms, the medieval Iberian world was dominated by the idea of *convivència* (*convivencia* in Castilian), of Christian, Jews and Muslims living alongside one another, respecting one another's customs, religious practices and laws. *Convivència* did not imply peace and harmony so much as separate communities rubbing along together. Under Muslim rule, Christians and Jews were second-class citizens, while under Christian rule the same applied to Muslims and Jews. When Tortosa was captured by the Catalans, the Jews and Muslims each had their ghetto (*call*). Tortosa prides itself on being the 'Mediterranean city of the three cultures', but this should not hide the realities of power. The town's giant processional figures (*gegants*) are four Christians, two Jews and two Muslims, reflecting both *convivència* and the realities of power.

Although it was the final expulsion of Jews from Spain in 1492 that has reverberated most insistently down the years, the fate of Muslim Spain did untold damage, especially to the south of Spain — Andalusia and Valencia. Twentieth Century Spanish school-books, especially in the Franco period, reduced *convivència* to one word — Reconquest. Yet there were areas under Muslim rule from the early eight century until 1492. Al-Andalus, the Arabic name for this world, was one of the great civilisations of its time, linking east and west, north and south. In modern Andalusia it has left great monuments, such as the Mosque at Cordoba, the Alhambra palace at Granada, and the Giralda, a minaret so beautiful that it was incorporated as the bell tower of Seville cathedral. Unfortunately in Catalan and Valencian lands there are no such grand monuments. Yet many of the great castles that dot the landscape have had a varied life as both Christian and Muslim fortresses, many of them changing hands several times before finally settling into Christian hands. Despite the lack of fine monuments, as sober a scholar as Robert Burns is moved to observe that Islamic Valencia was a 'paradise of advanced civilisation and luxury' for other Muslims.

Even New Catalonia, west and south of Barcelona, remained in Muslim hands until the middle of the twelfth century. Farther south, Valencia was secured by the Aragonese-Catalan crown in 1238. This means that in New Catalonia Muslim rule lasted for some four hundred years, while in Valencia and the Balearic Islands Muslim rule lasted five hundred years. These are not insignificant periods of time in the history of a land. Just as important, the date that a territory passed from Muslim to Christian rule is not the whole story. Until 1525, a Muslim presence was continued in the territories of the Kingdom of Aragon, and these Muslims living under Christian rule are known as Mudejars. Mark Meyerson's study of Muslims in Valencia during the reign of Ferdinand and Isabella reveals that by the fifteenth century, 30% of Valencia was still Muslim, against 20% in Aragon (i.e. the lands around Saragossa) and a mere 5% in Catalonia. But of course that 5% was concentrated in the southern areas of New Catalonia, and Tortosa and Lerida were both important Muslim centres. Following the union of Castile and Aragon, life became increasingly difficult for Muslim communities, and from 1525 conversion was enforced and policed by the Inquisition. Despite this, from 1525 onwards, groups of converted Muslims, known as Moriscos, continued with their own cultural and religious practices in private. The expulsion of the Moriscos between 1609 and 1614 was an economic, social and cultural disaster for the kingdom of Valencia, which lost 125,000 out of a total population of only 400,000.

The Muslims had been responsible for many important advances in agriculture, bringing new crops to Spain, but most important of all, advanced techniques of irrigation. They were also active in industry and trade, especially with the Muslim lands of North Africa. The expulsion of the Moriscos caused major disruption to the economic activities in which Muslims had led the way, and in the various administrative arrangements they had set in place to regulate the use of water for farming. The Water Tribunal still meets every Thursday in front of the Apostles Door of Valencia cathedral, as the Miquelet tower — once the minaret of the mosque — strikes midday, and is a continuation of that ancient Muslim tradition of the public administration of water policy and practices. It considers disputes in relation to the irrigation of the rich Valencian garden area (the *Horta*) that stretches miles inland from the sea and grows much of the region's oranges and lemons, flowers and vegetables. The novelist Rose Macaulay's description of this part of Valencia in her travel book *Fabled Shore* over half a century ago still rings true today:

> The road to Valencia runs smoothly through a plain of orange gardens and rice fields and other vegetable lands. It all looks smiling and fruity and very well watered by trenches and wells. The soil is red; their white houses are set in gardens of palms, cypresses, oranges, lemons, olives, carobs and figs. All pretty enough, but tamer, more docile, more utilitarian, than most of Spain.

In more Romantic vein, she was also deeply aware of the Muslim inheritance (she uses the terms 'Moor' and 'Moorish' which I have not used in view of their too frequent use through history as terms of abuse):

> Moorish engineering, Moorish castles, Moorish-looking minarets and domes, Moorish faces and songs, memories of Moorish battles against Jaime [Jaume] the Conqueror, who fought them all down this coast and hinterland and finally beat them and took their kingdom, but still they stayed on the land, and their Moorish-Iberian descendants now darkly and beautifully ride their donkeys along the roads, and walk gracefully from the water troughs with their tall Moorish pitchers on their heads.

* * * * * * *

The fifteenth century marked the high water mark of civic life in the kingdom of Valencia. Its iconic building is La Lonja, not a church or palace but the trading floor, the hub, of a commercial empire. The main hall, built between 1493 and 1498, and inspired by a similar building at Palma de Mallorca, has slim, twisted columns opening out like palm trees to support the vaulted ceiling. In Catalonia, the fifteenth century was more turbulent, and marked by civil war. Generally, the sixteenth and seventeenth centuries were times of unrest and sporadic violence throughout Greater Catalonia, and we shall explore this further in chapter 4.

Despite the union of the Castilian and Aragonese crowns, and the attempt by the ruling class to impose Castilian as the formal language of politics and culture, oppositional attitudes throughout Greater Catalonia burst into open conflict from time to time, and something of the separate traditions continued. There were the revolts of the *Germanies* (brotherhoods) in Valencia and Mallorca in the 1520s, and a major revolt in Catalonia against Hapsburg rule which lasted from 1640–1652. Pirates operating from North African bases ravished the coastal areas and the islands, and little Formentera became virtually uninhabited. Despite all these troubles, local rights and customs and the use of the Catalan language in trade and in everyday life continued to hold sway right until the end of the seventeenth century. All that came to an abrupt end with the War of the Spanish Succession. Both Catalonia and Valencia supported the Hapsburg candidate against the nominated Bourbon successor to King Philip II of Spain. England initially backed the Hapsburg cause, but later changed sides, earning itself the title of 'Perfidious Albion'. Valencia was incorporated fully into Spain in 1707. Catalonia was left to fight on alone, even after the war was concluded by the 1713 Treaty of Utrecht. Barcelona endured a long siege that did not end until 11 September 1714, the day now remembered as Catalan National Day.

1707/1714 marks the end of local rights in Catalonia, Valencia and the Balearic Islands, and the beginning of a process of rapid Castilianisation, with the Catalan language now regarded as a 'peasant' language spoken mainly by the poor and illiterate. The Bourbon project was one of modernisation and the power of the unitary Spanish state was integral to that project. It is also a period that marks a gradual parting of the ways for the territories of Greater Catalonia. From 1659, North Catalonia had been absorbed into the equally centralised French state by the Treaty of the Pyrenees. The French had arrived and were determined to stay, as witnessed by Vauban's great fortress at Mont St Louis (Mont St Lluís) at the head of the Conflent valley which dominates the fertile lowlands of the Cerdanya shared out between Spain and France. Menorca's history during this period is even more exotic. Valued mainly for the great harbour at Mahon (Maó), it was successively British, French, then British again, before finally becoming part of Spain. Mallorca and Ibiza, by contrast, were underpopulated and backward, still emerging from the impact of several hundred years of piracy.

In more recent times, this sense of being a periphery to the 'main business' of Spain is certainly a factor common to Catalonia, Valencia and the islands. Following the victory of the military rebels led by General Franco, the Catalan language was banned as a public language. Its sphere became the home, the neighbourhood. In Barcelona or Valencia, it became rare to hear Catalan spoken in public, and only rarely would a Catalan or Valencian address a stranger in that language. The novelist Carme Miquel was born in Valencia City and used Castilian at home, while other members of family spoke to her in Castilian. But older siblings, brought up in a village, used Valencian at home and Castilian in the street. She concludes: 'The same thing happened with all my cousins. The older ones spoke Valencian at home, and the younger ones Castilian. Let's say that those born before or around 1940 spoke Valencian and those born around 1945 already spoke Castilian. A similar thing happened in other Valencian families. Perhaps the language shift had happened before in some, and would happen later in others, but it certainly happened.' An acquaintance of the author was brought up in Barcelona in the last years of Franquism, by which time the family used Castilian at home. Now, on visits to her home city, she has had to get used to the fact that all the younger members of the family, born since Catalan autonomy, use Catalan at home. There were no newspapers, radio or television in Catalan, and magazine and book publishing in Catalan only became at all significant towards the end of this period (Franco died in 1975). These languages issues form the core of chapter 6.

It was in this context of linguistic and cultural fragmentation that Joan Fuster wrote his most influential and controversial book, *Nosaltres, els Valencians* (We the Valencians) in 1962. Fuster himself thought that he had produced a book on the social and economic history of the Valencian region to complement the kind of history Jaume Vicens i Vives had written for Catalonia. What proved controversial was the obvious intent of Fuster to emphasise the 'Catalan' nature of Valencia. Fuster himself admitted that in a minority of the Valencian towns and villages (*municipis*) Castilian Spanish was the normal language, and that for only 80% of the inhabitants was Catalan the first language. His claim that the 'important' places had always been Catalan-speaking was bound to stir up the inhabitants of substantial Castilian-speaking towns such as Villena in Alicante province, or the twin winery-towns of Utiel and Requena in the mountains west of Valencia, added to Valencia province by the Madrid government in the mid-nineteenth to facilitate the export of their wines through the port of Valencia. The key claim of the book, in many ways is this: 'Calling ourselves Valencians, quite definitely, is our way of calling ourselves Catalans.' Many of his Valencian compatriots disagreed.

Thus a book intended to bring together Catalan-speaking democrats throughout Greater Catalonia did not entirely meet its goal. Rather more successful was the Valencian singer Raimon, perhaps the best-known of those singers who emerged in the 1960s under the general badge of the *nova cançó* (new song). It scarcely mattered to those who heard him sing — in Palma de

Mallorca, Barcelona, Valencia or Paris — that he was a Valencian. It was not a matter of debate among the young people who attended his concerts, sang along to his records at home or were inspired into political activism by him, whether he called the language in which he sang Valencian or Catalan. Raimon brought together all those who wanted to end the rule of church and army, and the backwardness of Franco's Spain. An important recent non-fiction book by the Spanish novelist Antonio Muñoz Molina (*Todo lo que era sólido — Everything that was solid*, 2013) makes clear that this identification went beyond the borders of Greater Catalonia:

> In Spanish anti-Franquist culture, the glow of Catalonia and Barcelona illuminated everything. We listened to the records and went along in crowds to recitals of Catalan songs and to performances by Catalan theatre groups.

Of course, the reverse happened too. Paco Ibáñez's 'Andaluces de Jaén' (Andalusians of/from Jaén) was popular in Barcelona and Valencia. Indeed the words were by Miguel Hernández, a young communist poet of the Civil War born in Elche (Eix) but writing in Castilian. Ibáñez's own family reflects this 'general cause' in opposition to dictatorship: a Valencian father, a Basque mother and a childhood lived between France and Spain.

2. Factors suggesting divergence

If there are factors that support the case for the essential unity of the territories that make up Greater Catalonia, deeply rooted in the history and make-up of these lands, there are also factors suggesting difference and divergence. There are naturally two arguments here: the evidence from history, and the way that evidence is used in contemporary debates about how Catalonia, Valencia and the Balearic Islands should be governed. When Fuster described reactions to his book as 'hysterical' (prologue to the second edition of 1964) it was perhaps this distinction he had in mind. Writers appropriate versions of history that support their particular view of the world.

To begin with, there is the length of time during which various lands were under Muslim rule. As we have seen, this varied between insignificant amounts in Old Catalonia (Barcelona northwards) to some five hundred years in Valencia and the islands. We have also seen that after power passed from Muslim to Christian kings, substantial numbers of Muslims remained in Aragonese lands, with numbers increasing the further south one goes. Even after the forced conversions of 1525, the Morisco presence in Valencia was significant for nearly 100 years longer, giving a total of 800 years during which Islam was an essential ingredient of life in the Valencian lands.

During the process known in Spanish history as the Reconquest, there were heated quarrels between the crowns of Aragon and Castile, which often flared into open warfare. Inland from Alicante, the imposing castle of Castilian-speaking Villena and the equally imposing fortress at Valencian-speaking Biar speak not of warfare between Christians and Muslims but between the two Christian kingdoms. When they were not making war, they were carving up the new lands between them. So rather than a tidy border between Castilian-speaking Murcia and Catalan-speaking Valencia, there are anomalies such as Villena to take account of. Additionally, because the Aragonese forces included Castilian-speaking Aragonese and Catalan-speaking Catalans, the coastal areas where Catalan armies were most active tended to attract Catalan settlers, while the mountainous inland areas tended to attract Aragonese residents for the same reasons.

The events of 1519–1523, the rising of the *Germanies* (guilds), were complicated. There had been plagues in 1508 and 1519, floods in 1517. In the charged atmosphere following the Muslim rising in the Alpujarras in Andalusia in the 1490s and the increasingly vigorous activities of the Inquisition, it was almost inevitable that Muslims should be scape-goated. That this coincided with an urban movement in favour of local rights inspired by the ideology of the Italian city-states was, well, unfortunate. The revolt targeted both a perceived enemy within (the Muslims) and a perceived enemy without — the conjoined crown of Castile and Aragon, and its aristocratic representatives. A major military campaign was needed to quell the revolt, which was similar in many ways to the *Comuneros* revolt in Castile. It also spawned a rebellion in Mallorca from 1521–1523, in which only Alcúdia remained loyal to the crown. In Valencia the forced conversions of the *Germanies* period led to the decision that all remaining Muslims must convert. As had happened to the Jews, it was forced conversion that opened the way to the Inquisition (were the conversions sincere?) and eventual expulsion.

There were gains as well as losses from the integration of Catalonia and Valencia into the rest of Spain at the beginning of the eighteenth century. In particular these lands were now able to take part in the American trade. Despite the loss of many of the American colonies during the Napoleonic period, many Catalan traders made great fortunes out of the trade with Cuba, Puerto Rico and the Philippines in the nineteenth century. Miquel Biada traded guns in Venezuela where they were used to exterminate troublesome Indian tribes, set up the first steam-driven cloth mill in his home town of Mataró, and built Spain's first railway — from Mataró to Barcelona, opened in 1848. The textile empire of the Güell family was based on America too. Joan Güell, father of Eusebi Güell, patron of Antoni Gaudí the architect, began his working life in a textile factory in Havana, Cuba. And after various travels and adventures, including losing an uninsured vessel piled high (too high?) with goods for Cuba, Güell established a cloth factory in the Barcelona suburb of Sants. Now it is memorialised in the fascinating Park of Industrial Spain, next to the major railway station of Sants.

The industrialisation of Catalonia, and especially of the Barcelona area, was not repeated in Valencia. Instead, great strides were made in the improvement of agriculture, bringing more land under cultivation and introducing new crops. While the area devoted to mulberries decreased as the silk industry declined, that devoted to rice in and around the Albufera lake, just south of Valencia City, increased. In the mid-nineteenth century, oranges were introduced as a cash crop, and exported across Europe. In so far as industry existed, it was largely small-scale. Joan Fuster's guide *El País Valenciano*, published in 1962, beautifully illustrated with black-and-white photographs, reported fourteen thousand firms employing an average of ten employees each. Much of it was and is agriculture-based (for example the production of stuffed olives, *turrón* nougat and sugared almonds) though there are also extensive shoe, toy and furniture industries in Alicante province. This is the so-called Christmas quarter of Alicante — toys and *turrón* being essentials ingredients of a happy Spanish Christmas.

One of these small towns in Alicante played a major role in the politics of nineteenth century Europe. This was Alcoy (Alcoi), now more famous for its elaborate celebrations of the festivals of 'Moors and Christians' (Chapter 7). Here in the arid mountains, inspired by a local anarchist schoolteacher, the workers attempted to turn their adherence to the First International into practical action. For a period in 1873–1874 they declared the Alcoy Federation an autonomous, self-governing entity. It is an entertaining story, but should not for a moment turn our attention away from the overwhelming agricultural nature of Valencia. In terms of culture and identity politics, this proved of major importance. The great flowering of Catalan culture in nineteenth century Catalonia, the *Renaixença* (Renaissance) had only a pale reflection in Valencia. What renaissance there was in Valencia was imitative and did not garner the widespread support achieved north of the Ebro. At the end of the nineteenth century, this middle-class cultural movement in Catalonia developed into a middle-class political movement (the *Lliga Catalana*, Catalan League) which had no equivalent in Valencia or the islands. Thus whereas Catalonia pushed successfully for autonomy during the republican period of the 1930s, immediately preceding the Civil War, in Valencia it was an idea that only emerged in practical politics from 1936, by which time the republic, under military attack from Franco, and trying to deal with the exponents of social revolution in its own back-yard, had other, more pressing priorities.

Spain began opening up to mass tourism from abroad in the late 1950s, early 1960s. The Minister of Information and Tourism from 1962–1969 was Manuel Fraga Iribarne, and he is usually credited with the saying 'Spain is Different'. Years later he became 'different' too, re-inventing himself as a democratic, conservative politician who was President of the Galician Xunta (regional government) from 1990–2005. In saying 'Spain is different' he wanted to emphasise the great variety of landscapes, cities, historical and cultural remains within the borders of Spain, but without exacerbating separatist feelings. Political opponents agreed that Spain was indeed different — a military dictatorship in a backward economy at a time when Europe was moving forward rapidly in very different directions. Despite efforts to tempt tourists inland, the majority of visitors came for the beaches, in particular to the Costa Brava and Costa Daurada (Costa Dorada) in Catalonia, to the Costa Blanca in Valencia and to Mallorca and Ibiza. The impact contributed to both homogenisation — the beach holiday experience with perhaps a trip to a bull-fight or a flamenco club — but also to some differentiation. Tourists might begin with a beach holiday in Sitges, San Antonio (on Ibiza) or Benidorm but find themselves returning for rather more adventurous trips into the interior or to wilder coastal areas such as the Ebro delta or the saltpans in the southern part of Alicante province, or the less developed parts of the Balearic Islands. Travel writers started to use Catalan names for places, local food and celebration, finding difference where once there had been commonality of Sun, Sand and Sea.

The massive demonstrations in favour of autonomy held in Barcelona in 1976 and 1977, nearly a million people packing the Passeig de Gràcia, must have focussed minds in Valencia and the islands. Like the later pro-independence rallies of 2012 onwards, they took place on 11 September, the day when Catalans remember the loss in 1714 of their independent institutions. That sense of righting historical wrongs is central to the nationalist case. While a minority of Valencians and islanders were persuaded by Fuster's arguments in favour of greater unity between *Els Països Catalans* (the Greater Catalonia argument), for many others the notion of rule from Barcelona was as unappealing as rule from Madrid. Big Brother is Big Brother whatever language he speaks or address he gives. Anti-Catalan feelings did not just appear suddenly in the 1970s. Fuster in 1962 noted anti-Catalan feelings in Valencia which he put down to an inferiority complex. In a passage which accurately prefigured the mood of the Valencian Community at the turn of the century, he deplored what he called the provincialism of Castilianised Valencians who become great supporters of everything Valencian in response to criticisms from the Catalans, and also in response to criticism of their language from outside. Everything from landscape to Valencia Football Club was liable to be wheeled out in support of what he considered narrow provincialism.

It was in this rather heated atmosphere that a remarkable political coalition emerged between conservative *españolistas*, who thought of themselves first and foremost as Spanish, and more liberal Valencians who wanted to emphasise their regional identity but also their difference from Catalonia. The first success of this unholy alliance was at the time of the passing of the legislation that established the autonomous regimes for the various regions of Spain. While left-wing opinion favoured the traditional term *El País Valencià* (Valencian country), the centre-right argued for *La Comunitat Valenciana* (Valencian Community) — and won. Any suspicion of a reference sideways to the Greater Catalonia concept of *Els Països Catalans* was avoided. An early draft that contained the Kingdom of Valencia was likewise overturned. The other important concession required to secure passage of the legislation, together with the quiescence of the powerful military, was the clause that outlawed any federation between autonomous governments, e.g. between Catalonia, Valencia and the Balearics, or between Navarre and the Basque Country. For the moment, nationalism had been headed off.

The next substantial quarrel was over the flag. In general, Valencians had used the Catalan flag with the four red stripes on a yellow ground, but the centre-right from its powerful political base in Valencia City now argued for a version of the Catalan flag with a blue border, a flag which had been widely regarded as the flag of the city of Valencia. The Catalan word 'blava' (blue) thus came to provide the more vocal proponents of Valencian difference with their pejorative title of Blaverists. It was a flat denial of Fuster who had argued that 'It is not that the Valencian flag is identical to the Catalan flag. It is the same, the same as with the language and so many other things.' Not for the first or last time, it was Fuster's directness and inability to head off trouble that gave open season to his opponents. The language also became a political weapon, with political leaders rejecting the academic view that Catalan, Valencian and the island languages were forms of a single language. This argument culminated when Spain joined the European Union, with the treaty published in both 'Catalan' and 'Valencian'. Oddly, the two versions are identical. In the 1980s, what was initially a clearly Valencian movement soon morphed into a rather more clearly conservative, Spanish movement. The Popular Party was the winner, and turned Valencia into one of the most secure conservative fiefdoms by the end of the century. Vicent Sanchis describes this in disparaging terms in his 2012 book *Valencians Encara* (Still Valencians) updating Fuster on the 50th anniversary of the publication of *We the Valencians*: 'The People's Party has come to dominate power in Valencia (the *País Valencià*) in the same way as the most rubbishy of television programmes achieve the largest audiences.' Yet for many people, Sanchis was striking exactly that elitist tone that had so enraged Fuster's opponents and opened the way to the Blaverist version of pro-Spanish, anti-Catalan populism.

Similar pressures and tendencies were noticeable in the Balearic Islands. In general terms, a divided left made it difficult to construct a united front against the Spanish state. There were the Spanish socialists (PSOE), there were separate groups of Menorcan, Ibizan and Mallorcan socialists, all with more or less nationalist agendas, who might or might not at different times collaborate with one another or with the PSOE. Tensions between the islands were not new. During the republican period, 1931-36, proposals for a Balearic statute of autonomy had come a cropper because of Menorca, where some nationalists wanted an autonomous regime for Menorca and others preferred union with Catalonia. Similarly in the post-Franco period there was little support on the smaller islands for Balearic autonomy, which they feared would mean domination by Mallorca. Balearic autonomy was more imposed by the Madrid government than demanded by the islanders. Tomás Graves, son of the poet and long-term Mallorcan resident Robert Graves, has observed these tensions at first hand over the years. In his memoir *Tuning up at Dawn* (2004) he wrote: 'Most of the scant interchange between the three main Balearic Islands is for administrative reasons; otherwise each entity ignores the existence of the others, for the distances between them are almost equal to their distance from the mainland.'

The Balearic Islands are a geographical notion rather than a common history and identity. Some of the differences are obvious to the outsider, for example between the tiled houses of Mallorca and Menorca, and the flat-roofed, cubic, almost African houses traditionally built on Ibiza. Others are less obvious but extremely important. In the system of inheritance on Menorca, property passed to the eldest son, unlike the Mallorcan system of subdivision of properties. This means that Menorcan farms can still support a family, while in Mallorca tiny smallholdings have been abandoned as unsustainable, and the Mallorcan economy is much more dependent on tourism than that of its smaller neighbour. There is no real equivalent on Menorca of the bustle of Palma or the crowded, noisy brashness of resorts such as Magaluf.

At the turn of the century, the various island socialists, together with assorted greens and leftists, were able to construct a coalition to take power in the Balearic Islands autonomous government. A key plank of this Rainbow Coalition was an eco-tax (dubbed by its opponents the 'Tourist Tax') which would curb the damage done to the islands by mass tourism. The idea was a simple one: a tax of one euro per day on hotel guests, the proceeds of which could then be used on infrastructure projects such as cycle and walking routes, demolishing unsightly hotels and tidying up beaches and seafronts. There was massive opposition from the tourist industry and its associated business and property interests. All this uncertainty, coupled with a decline in tourist numbers largely due to problems in the German economy, made the tax very unpopular. The islands, long the most popular destination in Spain for foreign tourists, fell to third behind Andalusia and Catalonia. In 2003, the conservatives returned to power.

Public affairs developed very differently in Catalonia. For many years the Generalitat, the Catalan autonomous government, was dominated by the liberal nationalist governments of Jordi Pujol's CiU coalition. Pujol was a Catalan hero, jailed by Franco after leading a defiant demonstration at the Palau de la Música Catalana, Barcelona's wonderful *Modernista* (Catalan *Art Nouveau*)

33

concert hall, which included the singing of the banned Catalan national anthem. While in national Spanish elections, and Barcelona city council elections, large numbers of Spanish-speaking residents of Barcelona's working-class suburbs voted for the socialists of PSOE, in autonomous elections they tended to abstain, almost as if 'Catalan' politics were nothing to do with them.

The accession of Pasqual Maragall, the successful and popular ex-Mayor of Barcelona who had presided over the 1992 Olympic Games, to the presidency of the Generalitat in 2003 only served to emphasise the problematic nature of socialist politics in Catalonia. On paper, they were a separate party — PSC, or Party of Catalan Socialists. But in real terms, they were also the Catalan arm of a national Spanish party, the PSOE. Indeed the real winners of the 2003 election might be said to be the resurgent ERC (Catalan Republican Left), a 1930s party with a much more clearly articulated nationalist position than either Maragall's PSOE or Pujol's CiU. ERC and the United Left (IU, a coalition of ex-communists and greens) became members of a tripartite Catalan government. Maragall had hoped to renegotiate the statute of autonomy to give increased powers to Catalonia, and for a time appeared to have achieved this aim. But these reforms were eventually declared unconstitutional by a series of decisions of the conservative-dominated constitutional court, amid a frenzy of anti-Catalan feeling stirred up by the Popular Party and the media. By a series of steps which we shall examine in chapter 4, this brought Catalonia to the massive citizen-led pro-independence demonstrations of 2012 and 2013 and the 'illegal' referendum vote of 2014. ERC has continued to climb in terms of votes cast, even if its political position on many issues remains hard to fathom, receiving most votes of any party in the 2014 European elections.

Meanwhile, what of the Catalans north of the France-Spain border? In Collioure, in the shade of the great Templar castle, they dine early. Like much else, the

34

daily timetable has acceded to the pressures of the heavily centralised French republic. If Spain is learning to come to terms with double identities, for the French it is all rather new and rather difficult. The popular circle dance of the Catalans, the *sardana,* is danced as folklore to please the tourists, supporters of the two Perpignan rugby teams (league and union) wave red and yellow Catalan flags. There is change but as yet it is straws in the wind: an official 2007 local government statement in support of the Catalan language and culture; limited support for bilingual schools and for adult education courses in Catalan; the work of Joan Pau (Jean-Pierre) Alduy, mayor of Perpignan who won the 1993 mayoral election under the slogan 'Perpinyà la Catalana', and remained in office until 2009.

Yet North Catalonia played an important role in Catalan nationalist opposition to Franquism. Disaffected intellectuals and academics from Barcelona set up the Catalan Summer University in the town of Prada (Prades) in the mid-1960s. It was a place where both teachers and students could discuss the issues of Catalan life away from the prying eyes of Franco's secret police. It ran alongside the annual music festival established in 1950 by the cellist and conductor Pau Casals, who had sworn never to return to Spain while Franco remained in power. The summer music festival and the summer university have continued into the new era of democracy. The music festival is now a well-respected chamber music festival, while the summer university remains a true child of 1968, the year of its birth. But it has staggered on from crisis to crisis as an expression of the unity of the Catalan-speaking lands which some, at least, still feel.

3. A future for Greater Catalonia?

The truth of the matter is that, whatever the emotional bonds may be between the lands of Greater Catalonia, as a political project, it seems dead in the water. It clashes too obviously with other emotional attachments, such as that of Valencians to their own region, or the local attachments of the islanders. There are also attachments across borders, with migrants and the children of migrants still maintaining family and emotional links with other parts of Spain, or indeed with other countries. People are more mobile than they have ever been. Most obviously Greater Catalonia lacks any kind of political context in which it might be developed. Just as Scottish autonomy can now be seen as a step on the road to Scottish independence, or at least to a more federal structure to the United Kingdom, so the existence of the Generalitat in Barcelona, the Catalan autonomous government, has provided a context in which proposals to deepen and widen autonomy in the direction of independence can be developed and discussed. Conversely, conservative control of the Valencia Generalitat has made it a crucial base in the organisation of anti-Catalan feeling.

And yet, and yet. A majority of school-children in both Valencia and the islands choose (or their parents choose for them) to be educated at Catalan-language schools. Proposals brought forward in both autonomous regions in 2013 to revise the school curriculum, with less teaching in Catalan, and, curious as it may seem, the use of English not just as a foreign language but as the medium of instruction in some subjects, were greeted with great hostility by both parents and teachers. It remains to be seen how that particular debate will play out in the future. There are living and lively links between cultural communities in the various parts of Greater Catalonia, as there have always been. Maybe this is enough for people, but maybe people will want more in the future. There are complicated questions here of national identity, interacting in a variable geometry with left-right issues in politics, and the importance of multinational concerns such as the European Union and the various bodies that regulate international trade. The world may have become a global community, but perhaps as a consequence of that, people cling on to and even reinvent the local and the particular.

Fuster wrote in 1962 that where we come from is a starting-point: 'How can one be Catalan without being Valencian or Mallorcan, and vice-versa.' Or Menorcan, or Ibizan, or *Formenterenc*, or a citizen of *Catalunya Nord* (North Catalonia*)*, he might have added. For Vicent Sanchis (*Valencians Encara*, 2012) this remained true. Sanchis has done a great service to those thinking about these issues by reviving interest in a book by Joan Mira called *La Nació dels Valencians* (The Nation of the Valencians), a title inviting the question 'What 'nation' is this?' Mira contrasted Fuster's obviously true sentence about himself — 'I am a Catalan from Sueca' (a statement of personal commitment) to 'Calling ourselves Valencians is our way of calling ourselves Catalans' (a political project commanding only limited support). The leap in Catalan from '*soc*' (I am) to '*som*' (we are). Yes, writes Mira, being one day part of a future Catalan State is 'perfectly easy to imagine, would be very desirable, but is completely unreal.' Mira pointed out uncomfortable truths such as the fact that the Catalan-speaking territories of the Crown of Aragon depended on their loyalty to the crown rather than having specific relationships with one another. It was always politics from top-down rather than bottom-up.

Mira offered a challenge to the Valencians which applies equally to the other territories. He pointed out that we live with doubt and uncertainty in many aspects of our lives, but that this becomes a problem for a people who cannot come to a collective answer about the fundamental questions: 'Are we a people or are we not a people?' and 'What people are we?' Yet when he uses the term *convivència* to question how people with different and incompatible definitions of their community can live together, he perhaps forgets that exactly this term was used to describe how the three communities — Jews,

Muslims and Christians — shared the country together in the Middle Ages.

Yet what if all this talk of nations and nationalism, of autonomy and self-government are merely some rather weird mirror image of an essentially global and international world? Muñoz Molina, a Spanish novelist who divides his life between Spain and New York, is inclined to think so. He deplores the way in which the search for roots has penetrated downwards from Catalonia and the Basque Country into other autonomous regions: 'And in all these (communities), in imitation of Catalonia and the Basque Country, the myth was fed of a lost paradise, a primitive community that had managed to retain its identity unchanged down the centuries while at the same time opening up to the outside world and adapting to the changes of modern times.' In Muñoz Molina's view, Spain, by going for a universal system of autonomies, has ended up with an unwieldy, expensive and fragmented system of government. In turn this has produced the artificial, overblown and over-hyped fantasies of Seville's Expo 92, Barcelona's Olympic installations or the City of Arts and Sciences in Valencia City. It is time for a fresh start which reflects the interests of people at the grass-roots, of citizen movements which can break the present impasse of Spain's public life: corruption, conflict and political grand-standing. The book has sold well, but its practical outcomes remain straws in the wind.

An interesting contribution to the debate about Great Catalonia comes from Menorca, from Nel Martí who was an active member of the Menorcan Socialist Party and now leads the Més per Menorca (More for Menorca) group in the islands' parliament. He questions the statement in the Catalan Statute of Autonomy that 'Catalonia is a nation', since for him this ignores the historical, linguistic and cultural links between the different parts of Greater Catalonia. Yet he recognises that little is to be gained by seeing Greater Catalonia as a fragmented unity. He sees that unity being built, or rebuilt, from the bottom up, where people's sense of identity, of belonging to much smaller homelands, is the basis of some future coming together of peoples and cultures. He believes in a meeting and sharing of cultures that express difference but also shared values, rather than homogenisation. He refers to albums by the Mallorcan singer Maria del Mar Bonet ('Salmaia') in which she sings songs from many parts of the Mediterranean world, and Catalan singer Lluís Llach ('Un pont de mar blava') as examples. The title song of Llach's album ('A bridge of blue sea', words by Miquel Martí i Pol) expresses in moving, poetic language one of the most important concepts of this present book — the essential unity of the Mediterranean world, so strong in history, so weak in contemporary geopolitics. It is an area of cultural sharing, now problematic because of growing tensions between Christian and Muslim lands, and gross disparities of living standards between Africa and Europe. This is the main business of chapter 2.

Chapter 2
The Mediterranean

Both greater and lesser freedom comes down to the question of speech. And also of authority. To speak — to speak in the square — is our greatest dream. Both as dictators and as subjects, we Mediterraneans want to speak: to converse. So what about the sea? The free man always chérira *the square, the agora, the forum.*

1. The Mediterranean in history

When the Romans gave the name 'Mare Nostrum' (our sea) to the Mediterranean, they were not just making a point about the extent of the Roman Empire, covering all the shores of the inland sea from the Straits of Gibraltar to the coast of Palestine, and from Europe to Africa. The more subtle, implied point is the cultural sharing that has always gone on between the lands bordering that sea and the islands that dot its waters. Long before Valencia, Catalonia, the Balearic Islands or Spain appeared on the face of history, these lands were known to one another and to people from other corners of the Mediterranean — Phoenicians, Carthaginians, Greeks, Romans, Egyptians. Even in prehistoric times, the horizon where sea meets sky was not the limit of human ambition. One of the prize exhibits of the lovely museum in Mahon, on the island of Menorca, is a small, bronze statue of Imhotep, an Egyptian polymath, often called the Father of Medicine but equally associated with architecture and engineering, who was deified after his death. It was found at Alaior on the island and suggests strong trading links between the two ends of

41

the Mediterranean. Imhotep is shown seated, with a papyrus scroll across his knees, and this raises immediately one of the difficulties in understanding the old Mediterranean cultures: we know a lot about those cultures which developed writing, much less about those which did not. Yet to describe such cultures in negative terms such as 'prehistoric' or 'illiterate' does them a disservice.

The main culture of the Balearic Islands in prehistory is called Talayotic because of its characteristic watch-towers (*talaia* in Arabic). It was present on both Mallorca and Menorca, though it is on the latter island that the larger number of remains have survived. Usually the towers were associated with villages, some of them large in size, such as Son Catlar. Beneath the shade of the holm oaks, it is possible to spend a whole morning wandering around the large, fortified site. But whether the watchtowers were concerned primarily with defence, or whether they were concerned with government and public order within the settlement is a point that is still debated among scholars. This was not a static culture but one that evolved from numerous contacts with the outside world across the sea, with Greeks, Phoenicians, Carthaginians and mainland Iberians. Indeed Son Catlar was at its maximum extension in the years immediately before the Roman invasion. Agriculture developed, both livestock and crops, and social hierarchies were established. The body was made beautiful with ornaments, some of which can be seen in the Menorca Museum. There were religious rituals, associated with the *taulas*, tall slim stones with single cross pieces balanced on top. These religious enclosures existed both within and outwith the villages, and evidence of wine, animal bones, and deliberately smashed amphorae have been found.

Another find at Alaior on Menorca, also on display at Mahon Museum, was a statue of a young bull standing with curved horns and feet planted. The cult of the bull was certainly shared throughout the Mediterranean, but especially in Crete. We recognise it in the modern version of bull-fighting. This is now banned in Catalonia, but continues in centres such as Palma de Mallorca, Valencia and Alicante. Many of these events are aimed primarily at tourists, with local people preferring various forms of bull-running in the streets, stressful for the animals but dangerous, exciting and a colourful spectacle for humans.

The Talayotic culture should not be dismissed as local or unsophisticated, but it is certainly the case that there were people in the Mediterranean with greater aims and a wider reach. Menorca was not on the direct route that brought Phoenicians from the Middle East and the Carthaginians from North Africa to the shores of Spain. Ibiza, by contrast, was — its saltpans, still exploited commercially today, were of great interest to Phoenicians. For the Carthaginians, Ibiza was a vital trading hub, an important base on the way to their trading stations on the south coast of Spain. It was a centre for manufacturing figures of the Punic earth-mother goddess Tanit, described by Paul Davis in his *Ibiza and Formentera's Heritage* as 'the Great Mother Goddess, ruler of the earth and moon who ... encouraged passionate and erotic rites among her followers.' Rather crude small figures of Tanit were produced in large numbers, and 2,000 have been found in a cave at Es Culleram in the north of the island. Of more practical importance on Ibiza were the shallow salt-water lagoons at Ses Salines. From earliest times, salt was in demand for preserving fish, and salt extraction continued to be Ibiza's main industry until the arrival of tourism in the twentieth century. Sea water entering the salt pans is allowed to dry out in the sun, and is then exported, to be used nowadays for the winter salting of roads as well as its more traditional role of salting fish. The saltpans are also a nature reserve where storks, colourful flamingos and many other species of aquatic birds may be seen.

Such is the size of the Punic cemetery at Puig dels Molins, near Ibiza Town, that it was probably also used by notables from other Carthaginian colonies in the western Mediterranean. Ibiza was supposed to be specially blessed, not least in the absence of poisonous snakes. Bodies were interred in stone sarcophagi with many grave goods. The cemetery served the colony here for 500 years, and continued through the Roman period. It is now a World Heritage site. In subsequent periods, there was much looting of the tombs, but the remains on show in Ibiza Museum reveal something of the wealth of the colony and its trading links right across the Mediterranean world.

In later centuries, the Romans made contact with the islands, but wanted to do more than trade. On Menorca, they established important bases at what are now the principal ports of Mahon and Ciutadella. Inland, the Talayotic people absorbed Roman ways of doing things as just one more influence on their lives. Ibiza gradually metamorphosed from a Carthaginian (Punic) colony to a Roman one, as effortlessly as it had once evolved from a Phoenician to a Punic trading post. Eventually the Romans took control of the islands, and Palma and Pollentia (modern-day Pollença) grew as major towns. Where other cultures had been mainly interested in trade, the Romans stayed and eventually the islands became an integral part of the empire, if always rather a backwater.

On the mainland, the Iberian Peninsula had similar prehistoric cultures which through trade and settlement were absorbed into the wider Mediterranean world. In the southern part of the modern-day Valencian Community is the busy little industrial town of Villena. The town museum is small, exceptionally well organised and gives a clear record of this area in the years before Roman occupation. It was a turbulent zone of warring tribes, reflected in the quantity of military finds. A central figure was a female goddess figure, and a fine statue from the fourth century BCE is referred to as the Dama de Caudete (Lady of Caudete). Though some of the face is missing, she has the same complex hair-style and headdress as the better known Dama de Elche, a figure taken away to Madrid's Prado Museum after her discovery in 1897. The two statues were, however, shown together in Elche when the new Archaeology and History Museum was opened there in 2006. The exceptional elegance of the carving suggests the influence of the Greek world, a view supported by finds of both expensive pottery imported from Greece and cheaper copies made locally.

Only after visitors have admired the more routine contents of the museum are they allowed access to the great glory of the Villena treasure. Even then visitors are required to view a black-and-white cinema newsreel about the discovery of a horde of gold objects in 1963 in a gravel pit before the doors of the chest containing the treasure are thrown dramatically open and the gold revealed. It is thought all the objects came from the Iberian settlement of Cabezo Redondo but were taken away and buried hurriedly, perhaps during warfare. A heavy gold bracelet was found first, then the pot containing sixty objects, all gold except for three silver and two iron. The inclusion of two pieces of Phoenician iron, as objects of great value, dates this to about 1000BCE and the beginning of the Iron Age. Gold was a familiar material, mined and refined locally, but iron was a new technology only recently introduced and valued as highly as these glimmering golden plates and dishes. One additional item is an amber button from the Baltic, indicating the extensive trading links of these apparently primitive people.

The main site in Catalonia for considering the prehistory of these lands is Empúries (Ampurias) on the Costa Brava, an extensive area of Greek and Roman ruins shaded by pine-trees and fronted by a lovely beach. Two groups of Greek traders from Asia Minor (present-day Turkey) settled on this part of the coast — the Rhodians at modern-day Roses (Rosas) and the Phoecaeans at

Empúries. The problem is that we know quite a lot about these Greeks, but very little about the Iberian people with whom they traded. Again, it is the more literate who leave records, the less literate who slide into anonymity. The Iberian peoples of the Mediterranean coast of Spain certainly had writing, but only a limited range of inscriptions have survived, and much of the work of transcribing their written forms is very recent. There are no documents to describe their way of life, world view, or beliefs such as those the Egyptians, Greeks and Romans have left behind them.

The size and quantity of remains at Empúries reflect both the longevity of its occupation and the fact that this coast became prey to pirates from North Africa during the later Middle Ages, when the feudal lords of Empúries moved some miles inland to establish the small town of Castelló d'Empúries. Consequently the Greek and Roman ruins remained undisturbed for centuries. Whereas the Phoenician and Carthaginian settlements further south suffered because they were on the wrong side of a series of wars with the Romans, the Greeks at Empúries proved much more adept at staying on the right side of historical forces. They had begun life as refugees from the advances of the Persians in the sixth century BCE, reinforcing settlements at modern-day Marseilles, on Corsica and at Empúries. These wandering Greeks soon allied themselves to Rome. A Roman force landed at Empúries in 218BCE and subsequently established their main base at Tarraco (Tarragona). Initially the Iberians who shared the old town at Empúries with the Greeks resisted but they were overpowered by Cato following a second landing at Empúries in 195BCE.

The Roman settlement of Iberia that followed was a comprehensive colonisation. Latin replaced all Iberian languages (with the exception of Basque) and over the years developed into the various forms of 'Romance' spoken on the Iberian Peninsula. Many of the inhabitants became prominent in Roman life, including the Emperor

Hadrian who was born in Cordoba. The Roman town at Empúries is familiar in a rather comfortable way, with the forum a direct antecedent of the modern *plaça* (*plaza*) as a place for meeting and discussion of public affairs, and houses built around courtyards (*patios*). Even the temples seem to foreshadow little Romanesque churches in the Pyrenees. Hispania was linked to Rome by the mighty Via Augusta, which passed directly through what is still the main thoroughfare of the old town of Gerona on its way south towards the triumphal arch, the Arc de Berà, and Tarragona. The Romans built 13,000 miles of roads in what is now Catalonia, a remarkable figure considering that by the end of the nineteenth century Catalonia had only 15,000 miles of roads. Further south, the ancient town of Sagunt (Sagunto) a few miles north of Valencia City has a long and distinguished history from an Iberian settlement allied with Rome which fell to Hannibal in 219BCE, the important Roman town of Saguntum, and on into the Christian and Muslim periods of Valencian history. The fine Roman theatre and Arab hilltop castle are just two of the sights of modern Sagunt.

While it is not my purpose to suggest continuities between prehistoric cultures of the mainland or islands, or even between Roman Hispania and its successors (with the important exception of language), there are some general points to be made before we move on to consider shared Mediterranean features of the cultures of these lands in the last two centuries. Firstly and most obviously, the sea is a force which links geographical spaces and cultures as much as it divides them. While very few of the Iberians would have had the opportunity to travel to the Middle East, Greece or North Africa, these were not unknown places to them, but rather the sources of the goods they traded, the technologies they admired and attempted to copy, and beliefs which influenced their own attitudes to life. The old (Greek) town at Empúries was shared by Greeks and Iberians, each group maintaining at least for a time their own customs. For example, where the Iberians cremated their dead, the Greeks buried the bodies. Secondly, it is quite clear from the gold hoard found at Villena, or the sculptured head of the Dama de Elche that we do a disservice by using words like 'primitive' or 'barbaric' to describe cultures about which we have little written information, or only the reports of more sophisticated cultures such as those of Greece and Rome.

Thirdly, that landscapes can offer little or confusing evidence about history to the casual observer. Menorca is an interesting example of this. The landscape is littered with prehistoric remains of the Talayotic culture, about whom we know little. The island was under Muslim control from 903–1287, a period about which we have some written information but little if any physical evidence apart from over one hundred villages whose name begins Bini-. On the other hand, in the eighteenth century the brief wartime French occupation from 1756-63 left a rich legacy, such that these seven years seem altogether more significant than they were. The smart little town of Sant Lluís is named after the French Saint-King Louis. All the doors and shutters are painted green, a remarkable fact that seems entirely unremarkable to the locals. The French were also responsible for the bridle path (Camí de Cavalls) that linked the various look-out posts around the island. It is now being restored providing access to some of the most remote and beautiful coves of the Mediterranean. Yet to describe the French as more than a footnote to Menorcan history would be to exaggerate.

If we are looking for continuities, then rather than looking for ruins, it may be better to look for more subtle ways in which what we might call a Mediterranean lifestyle has been preserved in these lands. Most notably, the *plaça*, that sense of life lived in the open air, of a public space available for enjoyment but also for debate, for shows of power by those in authority, but also shows of protest by more humble people. Such are the musings we might indulge in at the great *plaça* at Balaguer in the foothills of the Lerida Pyrenees, where shops and cafes shelter beneath the arcades but also spill out onto the pavement or into the square itself. Or the tiny square at Ferreries on Menorca, used for markets, concerts or sitting quietly in the sun watching the world go by. Then there is Castalla in the hills behind Alicante, where the square shelters children playing beneath the houses and alleys of the old town which in turn shelters beneath the protective walls of an ancient castle. Such places are oases of peace, but in troubled times can become the scene of tumultuous public events. In recent years the celebration of Catalan national day (La Diada) on 11 September and the calls for greater political powers, for independence, by a movement based among the people of Catalonia rather than their political leaders, has been yet another reminder of the importance of public space in the Mediterranean world. Democracy, pleasure, culture; people making their own life stories, their own histories; the open air, the shared space. Such is the *plaça*.

2. The Mediterranean and the modern world

It all began at Sitges. The resort of Sitges lies south of Barcelona and is protected by the rocky headlands of the Garraf from the cold northerly winds which can blow for days on end from the snowy Pyrenees during a Catalan winter. For a hundred years or more, Sitges has been Barcelona's playground, near enough to be an easy day-trip, far enough to make the idea of escape a reality. If Barcelona and Valencia are the great cosmopolitan cities of Mediterranean Spain, Sitges is the place to live the Mediterranean spirit to the full. In winter it is a quiet backwater; in spring they lay floral carpets to celebrate the return of the sun; in summer it is a bustling holiday resort that claims to be the gay holiday capital of Europe.

Santiago Rusiñol was an artistic showman, a fine artist in his own right but a man who created an artistic milieu in which young artists and musicians could flourish, eventually making of Barcelona one of the artistic capitals of Europe. In 1891 Rusiñol inherited a couple of old houses in Sitges, on the headland dominated by the church. With his flamboyant fellow artist Ramon Casas, he collected a generation of artists and craftspeople, and eventually put together the collection now known as the Cau Ferrat museum. The collection includes two paintings 'probably' by the Spanish-Greek painter known as El Greco, but also work in wood and metal. Rusiñol was the first of the *Modernista* artists who believed in the integration of the arts and crafts and which found its flowering in the Barcelona buildings by architects such as Domènech i Muntaner and Antoni Gaudí. The Barcelona base of Casas and Rusiñol was a little café called Els Quatre Gats (The Four Cats, now lovingly restored and open as a restaurant). Picasso held his first one-man show here. The Catalan composers Isaac Albéniz and Enric Granados gave informal recitals here. The café embodied the spirit of the age.

After the year 1900, *Modernisme* in the visual arts made way for a new culturally much more conservative movement called *Noucentisme* (the art of the 1900s, but also a 'new art' since *nou* means both nine and new). It built on the work of the French impressionist and post-impressionist painters but without developing into the full-blown modernity of Picasso's cubism. A key figure here was the Sitges artist, Joaquim Sunyer (1874–1956). Cézanne, another great Mediterranean painter, had revived the classical theme of the nude in a landscape, and this theme of figures, clothed or unclothed, in a natural setting, is taken up by Sunyer. In a painting such as 'Composition with Nudes' (c. 1916) the Cézanne influence is overwhelming, including the angled foreground trees which frame the human figures. Better known and perhaps more typical is 'Cala Forn' (1917). There is a distant view of sea and coast, but the main interest is in the foreground figures (here clothed in simple, loose-fitting garments, typical of the modern, rationalist clothes then beginning to find favour in progressive circles) and their elemental still-life possessions — a *porró* (a long-spouted drinking vessel still in use that can be passed from person to person), a water-melon, peaches, a clay water-bottle. Such pictures and many more can be viewed in Barcelona's Catalan Art Museum (Museu d'Art de Catalunya), a gallery created by Gae Valenti over a period of ten years (1995–2004) from the over-bearing monstrosity of the National Palace on the Montjuïc hills above the city and the port. Sunyer created a new secular mythology which fitted in well with the spirit of resurgent nationalism in Catalonia in the early 1900s. But socially this was rather cautious, conservative nationalism, nationalism from above, one might say, in contrast to the popular and populist nationalism from below that flourishes in Catalonia today. It was a nationalism which turned its back on the noise and dirt and industrial unrest of Barcelona, in favour of the eternal values of the Mediterranean landscape.

The sculptor Josep Clarà, whose smooth, elegant, female nudes can be seen in various public locations around Barcelona (there is also one in Meridian Hill Park in Washington DC) was part of *Noucentisme*, a movement that spread through painting, the graphic arts and literature. There is little doubt either that the movement was greatly influenced by the archaeological excavation under way at Empúries and the various classical antiquities being uncovered. It is hard to imagine a greater distance than that which separates Clarà's statues, as cold as the marble from which they are made, from Picasso's heated, sexualised portrayal of the female form. The movement's claim to modernity was always rather empty. Picasso, the true modernist, had left Barcelona in the early years of the century for Paris, where he and Georges Braque were conducting their Cubist experiments. *Noucentisme* offered a sense of continuity with a classical, Mediterranean past, while rejecting the sentimental and the narrative, and aiming for clarity of form and content. Artistic tastes moved on, but this portrayal of the Mediterranean world with the eternal sea, the pine-trees, the olive-groves, vineyards and mountains, still speaks to us of a world that is so different from our own lives on the outer northwestern fringe of Europe, yet is also part of our cultural tradition.

Just as Picasso was not a Catalan by birth (he came to Barcelona with his family from Málaga as a young man) so one of the key artists of *Noucentisme* was a Uruguayan. Joaquim Torres-García (1874–1949) lived and worked in Barcelona until 1920. A typical work of his is 'Orange trees facing the sea' (1920), in Barcelona's Catalan Art Museum. The Mediterranean Sea provides the backdrop, the middle-ground is the Catalan landscape and the foreground contains emblematic figures, in this case two lightly clad women and a basket of oranges. The figures look out of the canvas and through the viewer, as if they are elements of a still-life composition. Unlike other *Noucentista* painters, Torres-García liked telling stories, and he used classical myths and legends in the murals that he executed using fresco technique in public buildings in Barcelona in the second decade of the twentieth century. Those in the Saló de Sant Jordi (St George's Hall) in the Generalitat Palace in Barcelona's Old Town can still be seen. They are politically significant too, not just in terms of Catalan nationalism, but its relationship with the other lands of Greater Catalonia. The group of young women in the centre are a symbolic representation of what it might mean to be Catalan — not just Catalonia itself, but also in the Catalan-speaking lands of North Catalonia, Valencia and the Balearic Islands. The giant male nudes either side of the door symbolise the manual and intellectual work of 'building a nation'. The popular title of this mural — 'The Eternal Catalonia' — makes precisely the link between history and modernity which was at the centre of this movement. For 'Eternal Catalonia' we might well read 'Greater Catalonia'.

Joaquim Mir was another painter who delighted in the light, the landscape and the colours of the Mediterranean world. A member of the circle of Rusiñol in Barcelona, the two painters went together to Mallorca in 1899. They returned, Rusiñol for extended visits, Mir to establish himself on the island where he stayed until 1906. Rusiñol loved the island and eventually wrote a famous book about it, translated into English as *Majorca: the Island of Calm.* He claimed that 'an island does not only mean land surrounded by water but the abode of peace, of illusion and of quietude; a repose for the soul and a resting–place for the wanderer; a camping-ground where we can halt before engaging once more in life's battle.' Here on Mallorca, painting the wild cliffs on the north coast, Mir developed a very personal style, full of vibrant colour, perhaps best exemplified in 'La Cala Encantada' (The Enchanted Cove). In 1905 he had a serious fall, and in later years lived in the area around Tarragona, eventually settling in Vilanova i La Geltrú, south of Sitges. Rusiñol's reference to 'life's battle' included not just the accidents of life but issues of social justice which were of great significance to another Catalan painter of this period, Isidre Nonell. He painted people suffering from long-term medical conditions or severe learning difficulties, and after spending time in Paris in the late 1890s, he turned to the gypsy community for his subject-matter. He expressed better than any other painter of the period, except of course Picasso, a generalised sadness which haunted the bohemian artistic life. Nonell, in his pictures of hunched figures in dark tones, achieved a real depth of feeling, a sense of the closeness of death and tragedy, and is the only Catalan painter of the period who approaches the tragic view of life in Picasso's blue period.

Artistic life in Valencia was dominated by one man, Joaquín Sorrolla (1863–1923). His life reflects a rather different orientation from the Catalan painters already discussed. As a young man he studied in Madrid and was steeped in the great Spanish painters, especially Velázquez. From 1890 Sorrolla lived mainly in Madrid, but travelled extensively, especially within the Valencian Community, in search of new subject-matter. The pictures which are most associated with him are the scenes of the Valencian seaside. Whereas in Catalonia, Sunyer and Torres-García populated their paintings with emblematic figures, and Mir preferred wild nature without a human presence, in Sorrolla the human figure is usually pressing up against the picture plane. In particular he loved to paint children bathing — the boys usually naked, the girls in light shifts — at the seaside, tumbling in the waves or playing on the sands, and although his taste may now seem rather dubious, he carried it off with style and panache. He continued to paint such pictures through his career, despite lucrative commissions from an international clientele, often focussing on mythological or historical subjects, and portraits. A bronze statue on a stone plinth at La Malvarossa beach in Valencia continues to look down on the sands and the children he loved to paint, and illuminated by that extraordinary light that pervades his paintings.

Oddly, one of the pictures that made Sorrolla famous is a rather isolated excursion into social conscience. 'Triste Herencia' (Sad Inheritance, 1909) shows a priest or monk supervising a bathing party of boys, several of them clinging to crutches. It refers to a polio epidemic which had struck Valencia a few years earlier and left many children crippled. There are the bodies, the light, the sand, the sea, all familiar from Sorrolla's joyous paintings of innocent childhood fun, but also a rather alarming reef of dark rocks, perhaps reflecting the perilous nature of human life and the way that disease can strike in the middle of a happy, carefree childhood.

Sorrolla's paintings are scattered throughout the world's art galleries, though a large number of them are collected together at the Sorrolla Museum in Madrid, his adopted home. In Valencia the Fine Art Museum (Museo de Bellas Artes) has a room dedicated to his work, recently inaugurated. His output was prodigious: an exhibition in Paris in 1906 included nearly 500 pictures, while at New York in 1909 he exhibited 356 pictures of which 195 sold. This show was at the Hispanic Society of America, and it was for the same organisation that Sorrolla painted a series of fourteen murals collectively titled 'The Provinces of Spain'. All but one were painted on location, hiring models to dress in local costume, and the work occupied most of the last decade of his life. The title is misleading, since the collection includes individual cities such as Elche as well as historic nations such as Catalonia. Elche is represented by (would 'reduced to' be too harsh?) a group of women weaving palm decorations under the palm-trees for which the city is rightly famous, while Catalonia has fisherfolk sorting their catch in the shade of pine-trees, with the sea a dominant presence, a very *Noucentista* scene. When the murals were loaned to Spain between 2008 and 2010, an unprecedented two million people viewed the murals in seven Spanish cities. Their success may reflect the general Spanish opinion that the particularities of the Spanish regions are more matters of folklore than urgent questions about daily life, national identity and governance. The Hispanic Society also owns some of the best of Sorrolla's seaside pictures, such as 'After the Bath' (1908) in which a woman in a light shift is about to be enveloped by a towel held by a figure of whom we see mainly her broad-brimmed 'Valencian' hat (something of a Sorrolla trademark) while the light shimmers on the water and creates bold shadows on the sand.

Two very famous modern Catalan painters also worked extensively at the seaside, in this case the pretty little fishing village of Cadaqués, just short of the French frontier. Salvador Dalí was a Catalan by birth, Picasso by adoption. For Picasso Cadaqués was a step along his way through life and art, for Dalí it was the centre of his world, and he settled at the nearby fishing hamlet of Port

Lligat, where his house is now open to visitors. Picasso visited Cadaqués in 1910. He had achieved the flat starkness of analytical cubism which confirmed the tragic view of life he had developed in his blue period. Cadaqués was the depth of his disenchantment with the world, but he chose to go onwards and upwards on a trajectory of re-enchantment that was to change the path of modern European art.

Picasso went on to puzzle and delight the artistic public for most of the twentieth century. Some years later, Salvador Dalí retreated inwards in search of enchantment. He took the everyday world around him but painted it in a way that re-invented both himself, the artist, and his relationship with the everyday reality. Yet very often his surrealist works are located in the hyper-real scenery of the Cap de Creus peninsula, not far from his home town of Figueres, the cliffs, coves, strange rock formations, flotsam and jetsam and the tumbling *maquis*-covered hillsides. If there is a beach and sea and rocks (the Glasgow 'Christ of St John of the Cross' in the Kelvingrove Art Gallery comes to mind), then it is this little stick of land jutting into the Mediterranean Sea.

In the 1920s, the Andalusian poet Federico García Lorca came to Cadaqués to visit Dalí. He had met Dalí in Madrid, at a time when Dalí and the film director Luis Buñuel seemed to represent the cutting-edge of Spanish, if not European, visual art. Lorca loved Catalonia, its language, its poets and its painters, perhaps hoping that he might be an Andalusian bridge between Castile and Catalonia. One suspects that the gay Lorca fancied Dalí at this time. The vain Dalí certainly thought as much, and later wrote as much. It is also probable that Dalí's sister fancied Lorca, and it is their friendship which we can imagine most vividly. She wrote of his charisma, recalling boat trips, sleepy afternoon *siestas* in shady coves, and the harsh heat and light of this unique landscape.

It is all a long way from the certainties of *Noucentisme*, or the shimmering light and innocent joy of Sorrolla's paintings of Valencian beach-scenes. As for Lorca, he was murdered by thugs in Granada in the first days of the Civil War, thugs who supported Dalí's hero, General Francisco Franco.

3. Tourism. The Mediterranean look north

A savage disregard for human rights became a badge of dishonour for the Franco regime, which lasted from the end of the Civil War in 1939 to the death of Franco in 1975, when his life support machines were turned off. The so-called 'nationalist' rebel forces had received significant help from the fascist regimes in Germany and Italy. Mallorca was the headquarters of the Italian airforce which flew regular bombing missions against Barcelona, Valencia and Alicante. The German airforce notoriously experimented with its saturation bombing techniques on the unarmed civilian population of Guernica in the Basque Country. Without such assistance, it is unlikely that what had begun as a military rebellion would have been successful. Franco was astute enough to avoid involving Spain in the Second World War. Instead he launched his own dirty war at home, eliminating or imprisoning very large numbers of his opponents, as we shall see in chapter 5.

For several years after 1945, Spain was ostracised by the international community. Some hoped for more direct intervention. They included the resistance fighters operating in mountainous areas such as the Pyrenees, featured in Guillermo del Toro's magnificent film 'Pan's Labyrinth'. Spain was one of the very few European countries which did not receive Marshall Aid. It was a by-word for all that was poor, dirty, backward and reactionary, an authoritarian state dominated by the military and the clergy. And yet the pull of Spain — the magical, sunny land where men and women of different cultures had

57

created a vibrant way of life that excited the peoples of Northern Europe — still exerted its force. In the 1920s and 30s, artistically minded men and women from both Europe and America had begun to settle on the islands of Ibiza and Mallorca. Driven away by the coming of the Spanish War in 1936, they now began to return. The Graves family, headed by poet-patriarch Robert Graves, was back in residence at Deià on the hilly north-west coast of Mallorca.

In Catalonia, John Langdon-Davies, who had reported on the Spanish war in the 1930s, came back with his Catalan wife, and ran a modest hotel at Sant Feliu de Guíxols. One of the first wanderers who came this way in the 1940s was Rose Macaulay, slipping across the French border in a battered old car, the epitome of the eccentric Englishwoman. She travelled slowly down the Mediterranean coast in a journey immortalised in *Fabled Shore* (1949). As Samuel Johnson had written in 1776: 'The grand object of travelling is to see the shores of the Mediterranean', a sentiment that Macaulay used as a head-quote at the front of her book. She reassured her readers that even in the heat of summer, 'In our time, a journey about Spain is not perilous, though it may be, and indeed cannot but be, romantic.' Rose Macaulay, a true traveller, always searching, seldom finding. The Catalans, Valencians and Andalusians she encountered were nothing but resilient, going about their daily lives, a great part of the time in the open air, as if their country had not just been torn apart by a great tragedy.

Twenty years later, in a rather wet Easter Week, I tramped the Costa Brava with two books in my rucksack — *Fabled Shore* and Josep Pla's *Costa Brava*. Things had begun to change. Pla and Macaulay described a wild and rugged landscape of cliffs and tiny silver beaches dotted with fishermen's huts that can now only be imagined by the visitor from the odd remnant of unspoilt coast that survives. Even by 1969, collections of fishermen's huts had developed into hotel and apartment block resorts. At

58

Canyelles Petites, beyond Roses, a single fishing hut noted by Pla had developed into what was then the latest urbanisation on the coast, a messy complex of half-built breeze-block villas and wild *maquis* scrub. The kindly owner of the local bar-restaurant, one of the first permanent houses to be built there, showed me photos of only a very few years before showing just three or four simple houses. Yet even in 1970, beyond Canyelles were the flowery cliffs towards Punta Falconera and Cap de Norfeu dipping towards the smooth, turquoise sea. In more recent years this whole Cap de Creus peninsula has been declared a protected site, and it is unlikely that further mass developments will take place along these cliffs.

Other areas have not been so lucky. The Costa Brava is a compromise. There are still enclaves that preserve that special wild beauty that gave its name to this coast. Other areas have been less fortunate. Lloret de Mar and Blanes, along with many smaller resorts closer to the great metropolis of Barcelona, have become the domain of high rise hotels, apartment blocks, and mass market package holidays. Many visitors have come away with only a dim idea of what Spain may be like, let alone Catalonia. The same has applied to Valencia, with its internationally famous (infamous?) resort of Benidorm, Ibiza (the resort of San Antonio especially) and Mallorca (Magaluf comes to mind). Yet the Costa Brava retains not only exclusive resorts, but also pleasant places for a family holiday such as Sant Feliu de Guíxols or Tossa, which have been able to balance the demands of modern tourism with the special coastal landscape which brought visitors in the first place. The same would apply to smaller resort towns on all the islands, of towns like Denia or Villajoyosa in the Valencian Community.

John Langdon-Davies wrote about the impact of tourism in *Spain*, published in 1971. He weighed in the balance the positive and negative impact of mass tourism. His conclusions make it possible to distinguish between serious concerns about the environmental and cultural impact of tourism and the snobbery of people who simply do not like big, brash holiday resorts, whether at home or abroad. Tourism had created an increased market for agricultural goods (and in retrospect paved the way for Spain's entry into the European Union). It had provided employment not just in hotels and restaurants and theme parks, but in the construction industry too. Langdon-Davies also made it clear that under the Franco regime, the inadequacies of Spanish tourism owed as much to the wiles of native sons and daughters, and inadequate government controls, as to 'offensive and loathsome' British tourists (Francis Kilvert's description of British tourists in 1870).

A balanced assessment scarcely describes one of the funniest and most original books about the impact of mass tourism along the Mediterranean coasts: John Anthony West's *Osborne's Army* (1966). Unusually for a novel (everything about his novel is unusual) it has a list of contents which also serves as a summary:

> Gradually the word spread. A deserted island: full of women: with free drinks. Amos Osborne had rediscovered the island of Escondite.
> His friends came.
> And the friends of his friends.
> And those who were not so friendly.
> And those who were not friendly at all.
> And ultimately:- Grockles.
> Osborne decided that action was called for.
> Action which shocked the world.

Escondite is a thin Caribbean disguise for Ibiza, where the author lived. Grockles are outsiders, strangers (here, tourists). The arrival of the grockles on Ibiza is prefigured half way through the story by a scene in Palma de Mallorca, where a character sitting at a café sees in one hour 'four street-hawkers with Toledo-ware souvenirs made in Minorca, two vendors of furry toys that jigged and danced when wound up, one balloon-seller; two separate women purveying fancy shawls and fans, a gitano type in torero hat ...' (and so on, you get the gist). Osborne eventually leads a revolt against the grockles and the tourist superstructure, destroying hotels and driving tourists into the sea. This final section consists largely of headlines in a variety of languages supposedly culled from the world's press: 'Guerra en el paraiso! Island in revolt! Kapitan Osborne: Alle Ferienganger 'raus!'

One of the characters in *Osborne's Army* is based on an English poet, Jack Beeching, who arrived in Ibiza before the tourist onslaught. He comes down occasionally to Ibiza Town from his rural retreat for a few days of conversation and drinking. If Osborne's novel is disturbing, *A Valley Wide* by Alexis Brown, Jack Beeching's wife, is a vivid and poetical account of a traditional community on the island at the point when its traditional way of life is about to disappear. She describes her first view of San Vicente: 'A half-hoop of grey beach, dotted with a few white houses, against a background of dark green hills. The sea in the bay was a shimmer of clear turquoise, darkened here and there to patches of violet where the bottom changed from sand to weed. To our left a narrow fertile valley, intensely green, marked out in meticulous pattern like a primitive painting, according to the crops.' Paradise indeed.

The positives of tourism were not just the economic changes outlined by John Langdon-Davies. Growing up on Mallorca, Lucia Graves observed the social impact of tourism was as great as the economic impact, even if its effects only became apparent after Franco's death. She saw it all at first hand, how the freedoms taken for granted by the tourists, especially young women, were observed and reflected on by young women, and paved the way for the dramatic impact of Spanish feminism in the 1970s. Her book *A Woman Unknown: voices from a Spanish life* (1999) speaks of the gathering sense of Spanish women of the injustice of their place in society, and (eventually) 'the war Spanish women were about to wage on their men, on their Anglo-Saxon and Viking rivals and on their elders. The Spanish women of that generation, educated on the doctrines of a crowd of moustached male chauvinists, began slowly to rebel, to change, to want what they had been told not to want.'

Perhaps today we take such changes for granted, as 'normal'. Of more concern today is the environmental damage created by tourism. The one major attempt to deal with this has been the Mallorcan 'eco-tax', and the failure of this initiative was outlined in chapter 1. In addition there is the issue of whether local identity is being lost, where tourism is in general a homogenising influence, where even local differences (customs, music, folklore) are subsumed in single terms like 'the exotic' or 'local colour'. Patrice Chaplin wrote about Catalonia in a novel, *Having it Away* (1977) which reflected Chaplin's own gradual awareness of the existence of Catalonia and its difference from Spain. The novel is about a small group of English tourists who scandalise the locals in a village on the Costa Brava. Throughout the English characters refer to 'Spain' and the 'Spaniards'. Catalonia only appears in the penultimate chapter.

Chaplin's own slow process of understanding is revealed more directly in her autobiography *Albany Park* (1986). Even so, only in the last third of the book, from the meeting with the real-life Salvador Espriu in Arenys de Mar, a small fishing village on the Catalan coast, do politics and Catalanism become apparent. Espriu had been born and lived most of his life there, she explains: 'I'd been reborn there so that was something we had in common. He said it was a magical place. I knew that too but didn't have the words to define exactly what I meant.' The poet and their mutual friend talk: 'Espriu had written a book of poems about Arenys de Mar, the happiness he'd found there. *Cementiri de Sinera* it was called. For him the resort was Paradise. But just one foot outside it was Paradise Lost.' Another character says of Catalonia: 'It could have been something once. The Civil

War wounded it and it healed up wrong'. The healing process continues, but has taken some unlikely turns, as we shall explore further in chapter 4 and 5.

Manuel Fraga Iribarne, Franco's Minister of Information and Tourism, was the man in charge of the uncontrolled blast of tourism across the face of Spain in the 1960s. He had no doubts about the benefits of tourism. In a 1990 press interview on Mallorca, looking back already a quarter of a century, Fraga claimed it had been a source of immediate wealth in a poor country, but also a strategic factor that had permitted other forms of economic development as well as widening mental horizons and getting 'our country' better known in Europe. Fraga refused to acknowledge the extent to which the uncontrolled capitalism practised by the young tigers of Opus Dei and their supporters inside government had precipitated a process which has spoilt visually much of the Catalan and Valencian coastline, and slices of Mallorca and Ibiza, unbalanced the economy by creating large numbers of low skill, low wage, seasonal jobs, and produced serious environmental problems in relation to water supply and sewage disposal.

In the development of tourism, Catalonia, the Valencian Community and the Balearic Islands looked north. That was where the money was, that was where the tourists would come from. Eventually the logic of economic development and the desire to preserve the democracy won in the 1970s would lead Spain to membership of the European Community too. In the process, Spain turned her back on the rest of the Mediterranean, on the Middle East and North Africa. Successive Spanish governments tried hard to cultivate good relations with the Arab world, emphasising Spain's historic role as a bridge to those worlds. But after the attack on the World Trade Centre in New York, and, closer to home, the Madrid train bombing, such sympathies became harder to sustain in a democracy dependent on public opinion and the next election.

And yet the rest of the Mediterranean is still there, and still waits. There are many problems: religious differences; the extreme poverty of much of the region; a profusion of unstable political regimes. Is it too much to hope that one day, the lands of Greater Catalonia which played such an important role in linking east and west, north and south, from prehistory through into the Middle Ages, will take up that challenge again? It is a thought we shall pursue into the next chapter where we look at the constant migrations that have affected the region, including the current situation where so many migrants fleeing poverty and political stability have lost their lives in the waters of the Mediterranean. The sea that divides, but also the sea that links.

Chapter 3
Population Movement

Every xenophobia answers another xenophobia since we are all foreigners to somebody

1. A preamble

I have already recommended a view of the Mediterranean which stresses the sea as a link rather than a barrier. It was the sea that made travel possible, and with travel went trade, population movement, the exchange of material goods, science and technology and, eventually, empires. In the previous chapter, I explained the importance of this in prehistoric times, coming up to the time of the Roman Empire. In this chapter, I shall show how it continued to be true for our chosen area through into the medieval period. Firstly in the eruption of peoples such as the Visigoths into the lands of the late Roman Empire, secondly in the movement of Arabs and North Africans into Spain from 711CE onwards, thirdly in the ambitious southerly spread of Christian kingdoms through the peninsula. Not forgetting of course the extensive medieval empire of the crown of Aragon, and the expulsion of the Jews in 1492, and of the Moriscos between 1609 and 1614.

2. The three cultures

The Iberian Peninsula in the Middle Ages was the home of three cultures: in alphabetical order, Christian, Jewish and Muslim. In order to give adequate weight to each, we must consider where these cultures came from, how they changed over time, the extent to which they intermingled and just how Spain and Portugal emerged from the melting pot as militantly Christian countries. Unified in the case of Portugal, but with a strong tendency towards fracture and disunity in the case of Spain. Within those processes of change, the main attention will be of course on what happened to the Catalan-speaking lands, while acknowledging that developments in Greater Catalonia can only be understood with reference to the potentiality of Spain.

The Roman province of Hispania was already Christian before the fall of the Roman Empire. The so-called barbarians coming into Europe from the east tended to acquire quite rapidly many features of Roman life including the Christian religion. In Iberia this gave rise to a well-developed but unstable culture under the Visigoths, initially ruled from Toulouse and later from Toledo. Terrassa, a textile town inland from Barcelona, was a bishopric from about 450CE, and an early centre of Visigothic culture. The cathedral, parish church and baptistery were built above the remains of the Roman town of Egara, and all three buildings still stand, though much altered. The little baptistery is probably the oldest and most evocative of these buildings, and demonstrates the importance placed on ensuring that the old beliefs were left behind, whether the gods of the Romans, or whatever belief systems the Iberians may have had. The Visigoths were Christians of a kind, but they were Arians who denied the doctrine of the trinity as expressed in the Nicaean creed. It was not until 589 that King Reccarred converted to orthodox Catholicism. Jews had settled in Hispania while it was still a Roman province and had been full members of society under the Arian regime. But from the beginning of the seventh century, strict laws were passed by the Visigothic kingdom against Jews, limiting severely their rights.

The one part of the Western Mediterranean that never fell under Visigothic rule was the Balearic Islands. The Byzantine Emperor Justinian extended control over the islands from about 550CE, but they never seem to have played more than a minor role in Byzantine affairs. Things changed from the beginning of the eight century when first the Byzantine Empire in North Africa and then the Visigothic kingdom of Hispania fell under the control of victorious Arab armies and their North African supporters. The inhabitants of the Balearic Islands were able to exploit the new balance of power to their own ends and from 707-902 managed to play off both Byzantines and Muslims and preserve a high degree of independence.

On the mainland, the conquest of Hispania by Arab armies changed substantially the position of both Christians and Jews. As people of the book, they were allowed freedom of worship and their own legal system by the Muslims, although in social and economic terms they remained second class citizens. The heavy weight of taxes bearing on the Christians of Al-Andalus (the Mozarabs) led many to convert to Islam, while others sought new homes in the expanding Christian kingdoms to the north.

Some of these matters may seem of limited interest. Their importance lies in the argument about at what point in history we can begin to talk about a country called 'Spain' and in turn the claim made in later centuries that Spain should be a unitary state dominating all the people of the Iberian peninsula. Some historians would trace the origins of modern Spain to the Christian kingdom of the Visigoths and the continuation of those religious beliefs and practices. But as Américo Castro pointed out in his major work *The Structure of Spanish History*, Visigothic Spain collapsed just at that point where it was most unified. The Muslims invasions left small groups — the Galicians, Leonese, Castilians, Basques, Aragonese, Catalans — to start as from new, 'each of them equipped with their own language and plan of life. From the crossing of their peculiarities would emerge the Spaniards' "dwelling-place" of existence.'

For Castro, Spain is born much later, in the rivalries between the Christian kingdoms, especially between Castile and Aragon, and in the intense interpenetration of Muslim, Jewish and Christian cultures over a 900 year period from the initial Arab invasion of 711 to the expulsion of the Moriscos. He has forced generations of Spaniards to confront the simple fact that in whatever branch of human culture we seek for evidence — science, medicine, poetry, personal hygiene, architecture, agriculture — Al-Andalus was more sophisticated than the medieval Christian kingdoms, while much of trade, industry and public administration was dependent on Jews. For Castro the origins of Spain are in that mixing of cultures in the Middle Ages, and this clearly has profound implications for what kind of country Spain might be today.

As Américo Castro suggests, the Muslims arrived in Spain with a clear superiority in most areas of learning and the arts. Wonderful buildings such as the mosque in Cordoba or the minaret known as the Giralda at Seville Cathedral are among the finest buildings in Europe. Unfortunately, there are relatively few buildings in Greater Catalonia which offer evidence of the splendours of Muslim civilisation. Gerona has its Arab Baths, but these do not reflect in any way the sixty years of Muslim rule in the town. Rather they result from an enlightened Christian ruler who wanted to copy the more sophisticated lifestyle of Muslim rulers. The Christian counties and statelets that were to eventually gather together under the tutelage of Barcelona can be identified only 100 years after the Muslims swept across Spain in the years after 711, but much of this area known as 'Old Catalonia' was under Muslim domination for 200 years. Further south and west, the lands of the Ebro valley and the irrigated lands around Lerida ('New Catalonia') were not conquered until the middle of the twelfth century. It was not until 1238 that Valencia and the Valencian lands down past Alicante were secured in the name of the kingdom of Aragon. In the same century the Catalans secured control of the Balearic Islands, again in the name of the King of Aragon.

Throughout these lands are castles that reflect a complex and often violent history. The state-run *parador* hotel in Tortosa on the river Ebro has been adapted from a castle that was once the Suda, the Muslim fortress that dominated the heights of the town. Under Muslim rule, the town boasted both Christian and Jewish ghettoes while a Mozarabic bishop in the eleventh century was employed as an envoy to the king of Galicia by the Emir of Saragossa. After the town was captured by the Aragonese-Catalans in 1138, fresh ghettoes were marked out for Muslims and Jews. Fortified as it was, Tortosa may not have had the splendour of Cordoba or Seville, but nevertheless shared equally in the life and culture of Al-Andalus. It had baths and mosques, poets and philosophers, scholars and musicians.

As might be expected, by the end of the Middle Ages and the unification of Aragon and Castile under the common rule of Ferdinand and Isabella, the Catholic Kings, numbers of Muslims in this area had declined but were still significant. Mark Meyerson's study of Muslims in Valencia during the reign of the Catholic Monarchs estimates that by the fifteenth century, 30% of Valencia was still Muslim, against 20% in Aragon and a mere 5% in Catalonia. But of course that 5% was concentrated in the southern areas of New Catalonia, and Tortosa and Lerida were both still important centres of Muslim communities (*aljamas*).

Muslim life in Valencia was very extensive and is deeply engrained in the culture of that area. Many words in both Castilian and Catalan for luxury goods are of Arabic origin, as will be clear on opening a dictionary at words beginning *al-* (though often the 'l' will have disappeared over time). Many kinds of fruit and vegetable were introduced by the Muslims, such as *albercoc* (apricot), *albergínia* (aubergine) and *arròs* (rice). Most of the words connected with irrigation, both its technology and management, are from Arabic. In government, both Castilian and Catalan use *alcalde* (mayor). Poetry and music were extensively cultivated too. So much has been lost, so much is hidden from us in our ignorance of the Arabic language. It is good that we can enjoy the heritage of Muslim Spain in more practical ways, in the gleaming fruit and vegetables growing in the irrigated market gardens inland from Valencia City or attractively arranged on the market stall, in the touch of a fine silk fabric (one of Valencia's most traditional products) and in the spiced pastries at the local baker's shop. Or, as I mentioned, by witnessing the weekly Water Tribunal held in front of Valencia cathedral and remembering that it was Muslims who taught Spain how to use one of its most precious resources — water.

As we have seen, the Jews enjoyed both rights and privileges in the Visigothic kingdom at least until the change from Arian to Catholic beliefs. The Jewish *aljamas* or *calls* (ghettoes) also enjoyed rights and privileges under Muslim rule. They acquired Arabic as a language of translation (although they usually wrote it using Hebrew script) and through their knowledge of Arabic acquired a knowledge of and interest in philosophy and poetry. It was from the Muslims, as Castro reminds us, that Christian rulers in Spain learned 'the art of utilizing the Jews as physicians, scientists, tax-collectors, public officials, diplomats, and, in general, as administrators of the wealth of the state and of the nobility.' Like the Mozarabs, they suffered from persecution by the Almohads and Almoravids, fundamentalist Muslims who arrived from North Africa in the twelfth century as the caliphate in Cordoba broke up into a patchwork quilt of local states (*taifas*). Many of the Jews fled to Christian kingdoms, which likewise became very dependent on them.

The years between 1200 and 1400 mark the peak of Jewish life in Greater Catalonia. Barcelona and Perpignan were both important Jewish centres, as was Gerona, but there were also Jewish *calls* in smaller Catalan towns such as Besalú, La Bisbal and Olot. Probably up to 5% of the population of Catalonia, some 10,000-12,000 people, were Jewish, while in urban centres the proportion rose to 10%. Robert Burns (*Muslims, Christians, and Jews in the Crusader Kingdom of Valencia*) puts the figure as high as 25,000, and all such figures should be treated with caution! The Jews were given special protection by kings and nobles, who often referred to 'my' Jews, and the *call* was usually close to the centre of civil and/or ecclesiastical power. The Gerona *call* lay either side of the main street, the Carrer de la Força in the old town, a jumble of narrow little alleyways and tall dark houses that now house an excellent museum. In Valencia, there were major Jewish *aljamas* in Valencia City, Castellon, Xativa and Sagunt. By the end of the thirteenth century, according to Burns, there were probably 50,000 Jews in Valencia and 140,000 Muslims, compared with only 50,000 Christians.

The Jews in medieval Catalonia and Valencia were active in a wide variety of trades, crafts and professions. They were tailors, curtain-makers, cobblers, silversmiths, bankers, doctors and midwives. Like the Muslim population of Christian kingdoms, the Jews had their own legal structure, and in many documents Muslim and Jewish communities are described as 'laws' rather than religious or ethnic groups. Every time we read about a government decree banning Jewish participation in a particular trade or profession, this is clear evidence that Jews were following that particular calling: for example, in 1326 Jews in Barcelona were banned from selling missals with pictures of saints. However, Castro may exaggerate when he claims that Jews always emphasised the practical uses of learning. Gerona in particular was a focus of interest in the Cabbala which proposed, in essence, an interpretation of the Hebrew Bible (the Old Testament) quite as mystical as the work of Muslim Sufis or (later) Christian poets such as St John of the Cross. This esoteric tradition was probably the result of influences from Jewish communities in Provence, many of whom fled south at this time in the face of persecution.

It is an extraordinary historical shift which runs from a position where the activities of Jews were contributing far above their numbers to the economic and political power of Aragon, to the pogroms of 1391 and one hundred years later, the expulsion of 1492. Increasingly, Christian clerics, led by the Dominican order and preachers such as the Valencian Vicent Ferrer, pressed the Jewish community to recognise the superiority of the Christian religion. It was the 'alternative' Pope (Benedict XIII — 'Papa Luna') who established the Disputation of Tortosa which lasted from February 1313 through into 1314. No doubt Papa Luna saw it as a late attempt to gain popular support from his base in the fairy-tale seaside castle at Peniscola between Castellon and Tortosa. Jews were compelled to attend, and all but two of their rabbis converted, which in turn led to mass conversions and persecutions of those who did not convert. There is little doubt that in the European mind after the horrors of the Black Death, there was a compulsive reaching out to identify a scapegoat, and the Jews were at hand, easily identifiable from where they lived and how they dressed. In the hundred years between 1391 and 1492 there was a dramatic reduction in the number of Jewish *aljamas* throughout the Aragonese lands. In Catalonia, 25 communities in 1391 had become 14 by 1419 with only a fraction of the population.

Those Jews who converted were in a cleft stick. They had renounced their religion, but since they continued with cultural practices and maintained contact with friends and family members who had not converted, they were continually suspected of secretly clinging to their religion. Ferdinand was also in a cleft stick. His marriage to Isabella of Castile had united the crowns but there were major policy differences. In particular, Aragon feared the impact on the economy of harsh measures against the Jews and Muslims. Ferdinand resisted the extension of the Inquisition to Aragonese lands, but in retrospect was swimming against the tide of history. The new Spain that had been created by the merging of the two crowns was to become the spearhead of militant Christianity in Europe. It was the beginning of what Castro calls the 'regressive rhythm of Hispanic history'. In later centuries Spaniards looked back to the Good Old Days of Isabella and Ferdinand, but the seeds of the narrow intolerance of the Dominicans were already bearing fruit by the end of the fifteenth century.

Ferdinand continued to use Jewish financiers and administrators right up until the final expulsion of the Jews in 1492. Once there had been forced conversions, there was no looking back: those who had converted were always suspected of back-sliding, of being Catholic in public and Jewish in the privacy of their own homes. Gossip and slander were used widely by the Inquisition as evidence; a number of the leading clerics of the Inquisition were themselves converts and this fact seemed to give them a particular enthusiasm for the task. Religious motives were entwined with economic motives, especially the confiscation of Jewish property. So in Gerona, between 1489 and 1505, no fewer than fourteen members of the wealthy Falcó family suffered the attentions of the Inquisition. By 1495 the City Council of Barcelona was complaining to King Ferdinand that after years of civil war, almost the only economic activity taking place in the city was in the hands of converts, some of whom were fleeing in fear of the Inquisition. Whatever hopes the Catalan economy might have had of recovery, within the new Spain turning to face the Atlantic and America, they were certainly not helped by persecution of those suspected of holding to Judaism in their hearts.

One particular case in Valencia shines further light on the particular interest that the Inquisition took in Jewish converts. Luis Vives was one of the great humanist scholars of the sixteenth century. He was from Valencia and is remembered there by a splendid statue dominating the university patio. Yet he left Valencia for the life of a wandering scholar (Paris, Oxford and Bruges) and did not return. Joan Fuster suggests rather timidly that this *may* possibly have been because of Jewish family members and fear of the Inquisition, but bearing in mind that family members had been killed at the hands of the Inquisition, this seems highly probable. Both his Jewish family and his unorthodox religious views made him a potential target for the Inquisition.

Ferdinand was forced to back down over the Jewish question, but was more successful with the Muslims who, as we have seen, continued to be a significant proportion of the population of the Valencian lands. The conquest of Granada by Castile in 1492 meant the end of Al-Andalus. Some Muslims remained but following a rising in the Alpujarras (between Granada and the sea) all the Mudejars of Andalusia and Castile were offered the choice of exile or conversion. On conversion they became known as Moriscos, and like Jewish converts were prey to the Inquisition. This decree did not apply to the Aragonese lands, but the issue of community relations became embroiled in the popular uprisings that broke out in Valencia and Mallorca in 1520, known as the revolt of the *Germanies* (brotherhoods). As we shall see below, a combination of popular pressure from within and external pressure from Castile led to forced conversions in all the Aragonese territories.

But first, there are further comments to be made about the significance of the Muslim heritage in the Valencian Community, and also about the Christian soldier of fortune Ruy Díaz, who has come down to us in myth and legend and a very little history as El Cid. The written version of the epic poem which is the main source for his story refers to events in the 1080s and 1090s. At this time not only were the Christian kingdoms involved in considerable squabbles between themselves, but the unified government of Al-Andalus under the authority of the Cordoba caliphate had given way to a considerable number of statelets (*taifas*) each with its own ruler. Thus the poem is not strictly an account of Muslims doing battle with Christians, but a complex pattern of disorder in which El Cid fights as often for Muslim rulers as for Christians, his enemies including no less a personage than the Count of Barcelona! One thing we can glean from the poem is the wealth of Valencia City. When El Cid conquers the city, 'there were untold quantities of gold and silver, all who took part became rich.' One of El Cid's first actions is to take his men up to the highest point of the fortress, from where 'they saw how the city of Valencia lay before them, with the sea on one side and on the other the wide, luxuriant plantations of the *Huerta*.' It would be 1238 before James I (Jaume I) 'the Conqueror' finally secured control of Valencia. Many Muslims were resettled south of the River Xúcar, so that the rich, irrigated lands of the *Huerta* (*Horta*) admired by El Cid and his men could be handed over to Catalan and Aragonese settlers. In the city, Muslim craftsmen and their families were resettled in the *moreria*, a separate walled area. It is difficult to visit the Valencian Community and not be aware of those long centuries of Muslim culture, both when they controlled the territory and in later years as subjects of the Aragonese crown.

Although there was cultural mingling and no doubt some racial mingling too, the last century of Muslim presence in Valencia was not a happy one. While the Mediterranean policy of the Catholic Kings centred increasingly on a clash between Islamic East (the rising power of the Ottoman Empire) and Christian West, Ferdinand's home policy continued to recognise the Muslims of the old Kingdom of Aragon as a hard-working sector of society. When the clash came, it came from below. In 1519–1523 there was an explosion of rage in Valencia (copied on Mallorca from 1521–1523) against feudal power, and in favour of local rights, occasioned by the departure of the new King of the combined kingdom, Charles I, to be Holy Roman Emperor. A similar movement in Castilian towns was known as the revolt of the *Comuneros*. But a particular feature of the *Germanies* in Valencia, a movement centred among the urban craft guilds, was that as the months passed, it became an anti-Muslim movement. While Christians and Muslims had often socialised together in the past, a matter of concern to King Ferdinand, the Christians now turned against their Muslim neighbours. This in turn led to forced conversion and as we saw in the case of the Jews, as soon as there was forced conversion, there was also doubt as to the reality of those conversions. The result was that Valencian Muslims were offered the same choice as had been made to Castilian and Andalusian Muslims twenty years before: conversion or exile. Some chose to leave, but many remained. Converts the Moriscos may have been, but Mudejars and Muslims they remained. As Mark Meyerson writes in *The Muslims of Valencia in the Age of Fernando and Isabel*: 'Social structures and mores, family life — even feuding — an Arabic culture, and religious belief all lent the Mudejars a sense of distinctiveness, tradition, and pride which the baptismal waters could not erase.' When the Moriscos were expelled from Spain, including the Aragonese lands, between 1609 and 1614, it was a cultural and economic disaster. Fuster calculates that 125,000 out of a population of 400,000 in Valencia emigrated. Most of them went to North Africa, lands with which they had always had strong cultural and trading links.

Relations between Muslims and Christians in the Balearic Islands developed in rather different ways. The conquest of Menorca can only be described as ethnic cleansing but on Mallorca, following an initial bout of pillaging by Jaume's army, in which many inhabitants were either killed or taken to be sold as slaves, it seems clear that the conquest of 1229 had an element of negotiation about it, with some large Muslim landowners allowed to keep their land. Mallorca was the base of one of the major philosophers of the Middle Ages, Ramon Llull (Raymond Lully). He travelled widely in the Muslim world and wrote in Arabic as well as Latin and Catalan. If Catalan princes and merchants wanted to conquer the Mediterranean by force of arms, Llull harboured a more ambitious project: to reunite Islam and the Jews with Christianity by force of argument and logic.

We have already observed Castro's view that most educated Jews stressed the practical outcomes of learning. One Mallorcan Jew who exemplifies this is Cresques Abraham (sometimes confusingly referred to as Abraham Cresques). He was a famous cartographer who drew the beautifully illustrated Catalan Atlas of 1375. His son Jehufa (or Jafuda) followed the same profession, and is remembered by a statue in the old Jewish *call* of Palma. Despite this veneer of tolerance, the Mallorcan Jews were a particular target for militant Christians. Jehufa was one of many who converted after the pogrom of 1391. In 1413 the Valencian Saint Vincent Ferrer preached against the Jews in Mallorca, and the remaining two hundred converted after an unholy episode in 1436, when sixteen Jews were arrested and accused of sacrilege. Four — leaders of the *aljama* — accepted conversion rather than death by burning and the city authorities then let it be known that they would escape death completely if the rest of the Jewish community converted. It was agreed, and a solemn *Te Deum* sung in the Cathedral at Palma.

Thus officially there were no Jews on Mallorca in 1492, the year of the expulsion. Over the years, the converts, *Xuetes* as they came to be known on the island, especially after active persecution ceased, became a feature of the life of Majorca. 99 of them perished at the hands of the Inquisition between 1489 and 1535 but many others continued to live publicly as Christians and secretly as Jews. We know little enough of their religious, cultural or social life, but there was sufficient evidence for 37 of them to be burned in 1691, although the balance of economic jealousy and religious motives is hard to estimate. Despite the attempt by enlightened Spanish monarchs to regularise their position at the end of the eighteenth century, an element of social stigma continued to attach to these families, ignorant of Judaism, yet still paying for the supposed 'blood guilt' of their Jewish ancestry.

In recent times, there has been less active discrimination against *Xueta* families. Robert Graves thought that by the middle of the twentieth century, these families numbered some three hundred. In the new democratic post-Franco world there has been more open discussion of the fate of the Sephardic Jews, and there are once again synagogues, both orthodox and reform, in the major centres of population in Greater Catalonia. Jews from other countries have become more willing to visit and settle in Spain, including Mallorca. As for the *Xuetes*, a number have re-converted to Judaism, and there are contacts with Israel.

3. *Convivència* and the realities of power

Convivència is the Catalan term for the circumstances under which Christians, Jews and Muslims lived in relative harmony during long periods of the Middle Ages. The major influence here was the tradition of tolerance in Islam, as Américo Castro has emphasised. Llull on Mallorca managed to link a stated aim to re-unite the three religions (ostensibly by persuading Jews and Muslims of the truth of Christianity) with a deep knowledge of and interest in Islam, especially the mystic tradition of Sufism. He was influenced by the Murcian Sufi Ibn Arabi, who wrote:

> My heart can take on any form: it is a pasture for gazelles and a monastery for Christian monks.
> A temple for idols, and for the Kaaba of the pilgrims, and for the tables of the Torah, and for the book of the Koran.

> I follow the religion of love: whatever the direction of the
> camels of my love, my religion and faith are there.

Unfortunately, it is not in general men like Llull or Ibn
Arabi who direct the spiritual and temporal affairs of this
world. Tolerance was a *modus vivendi*, a rubbing along
together, a fact of everyday life, rather than a doctrine or
policy promoted by civic and religious leaders. I emphasise 'civic and religious' because it was precisely the lack
of a clear line between one and the other in all three
communities that stoked the fires of intolerance. Whether
this was the exclusivism and separateness of Jews, the
hot-headed Almoravids and Almohads who wanted to
return Islam to what they saw as a purer, proselytising
religion, or the Pope and the religious orders (Dominicans
especially), there were many who viewed life in a more
neatly compartmentalised form than had been the habit
during the long years of *convivència*. Just as Christians
and Jews had 'known' their place under Muslim rule, so
Muslims had to learn their place in Christian society.
Burns notes in his excellent study of Muslim/Christian/
Jewish relations in Valencia that within one hundred
years of the conquest, 'Christian settlement would have
pushed the Muslims out of this paradise into the non-irri-
gated or dry-farming zones.'

A further reality that affected Muslim-Christian relations in the Western Mediterranean was the ubiquity of
piracy. While this had existed in the Middle Ages, piracy
and hostage-taking became even more widespread in the
fifteenth and sixteenth centuries. Piracy was an integral
part of the fluctuating, interlocking cultural and
economic system of the Mediterranean, part of the restless tide of human activity across the tideless sea. The
conquest of Mallorca by the Catalans was a specific
response to piracy. As early as the thirteenth century, the
English chronicler Matthew Paris wrote that Mallorca
was 'crammed with pirates and robbers'. As well as
casual piracy, there were privateers who operated with

79

licence from a ruler. This led to diplomatic incidents, as for example when James I the Conqueror made an alliance with Tunis, but Catalan pirates continued to attack shipping operating out of Tunis. Like war, piracy was an extension of commercial conflict. It might be between Christian states or between Muslim states as well as between Muslims and Christians. The relatively small number of seaside settlements in Greater Catalonia, before the twentieth century tourist boom, bears witness to the insecurity of coastal areas.

4. Aragonese and Spanish empires

When contemporary Valencian politicians accuse their neighbours in Catalonia of imperialism, this is not without some basis in history. Catalonia has been a colonial power twice — in the Middle Ages operating under the banner of the Crown of Aragon, and in the nineteenth century doing business as part of Spain.

Even after the marriage of the Count of Barcelona and the Queen of Aragon in 1137 which united the two political powers of north-east Spain, economic and cultural ties north of the Pyrenees (and beyond what we have come to know as North Catalonia) continued to be important to the Catalans. Provençal was the language of poetry and romance. But in 1212 King Peter of Aragon (Pere I) was defeated by a bloodthirsty, crusading army led by Simon de Montfort at the battle of Muret. De Montfort had two aims both of which were achieved: first to wipe out the Cathars (the Albigensian heresy) and secondly to extend the power of the Counts of Toulouse in alliance with the French crown at the expense of the Count of Barcelona. From this time on, Aragonese and Catalan attention turned south and east, to the conquest of Muslim lands in Valencia, and the acquisition of territories, trade and influence across the Mediterranean world.

Robert Hughes' book *Barcelona* has an inapt title, as it is one of the best summaries in English of Catalan history and art. Hughes does not mince his words about the medieval Catalan empire. He was well liked in Barcelona, but he pulls no punches, describing as 'cultural genocide' what happened when the Catalans arrived in Menorca and Sardinia. He describes how King Alfons II (the Liberal!) invaded Menorca in 1287, slaughtered most of its male population and sold the rest as slaves. It took Menorca two hundred years to recover from this experience. Some Catalan nationalists take great pride in the fact that people in the Sardinian town of Alghero (l'Alguer in Catalan) still speak a Catalan dialect. This is only so because Peter III (Pere III) executed or drove into exile the original inhabitants and replaced them with Catalan settlers.

Early in the fourteenth century Catalan pirates (with official support) attacked the Byzantine Empire and for many years controlled the Duchy of Athens. We have a good contemporary account of this in the *Chronicle* of Ramon Muntaner, written in Catalan but available in English translation, and in Alfonso Lowe's curiously named *The Catalan Vengeance.* Lowe's book describes events that took place between 1302 and 1311, and again the word piracy is not so far from the mark. The Catalan Company, of which Muntaner was a member, sought to supplement earnings from trade in the eastern Mediterranean with booty. They were referred to as the Almogavars, from an Arabic word meaning raiders. Led by Muntaner's hero, Roger de Flor, the Catalans and their cronies planned to carve out for themselves a commercial empire in Asia Minor. All went well at first, but following the murder of Roger de Flor, the Catalans set out on a murderous path of vengeance, slaughtering and burning their way through Macedonia and other parts of Byzantium-in-Europe. Eventually they settled in the backwater of Athens where they continued to control the Duchy until 1388, by which time they were a severe embarrassment to the crown of Aragon. Legitimate trade could sometimes be less costly than involvement in dynastic and territorial squabbles.

If the activities of the Catalan Company represented the unacceptable face of Aragonese imperialism, in other ways the Catalans were a model for decorum and peaceful trading. Barcelona, Valencia and Palma de Mallorca were all important international centres, where merchants, bankers and traders were the main beneficiaries of expansionist foreign policies. In some cases, conquest confirmed existing trading links; in others it created fresh opportunities. This trade was regulated by consulates in all the major Mediterranean towns, including in North Africa, and by the code of commercial and maritime practice consolidated in mid-fourteenth century Barcelona and known as the *Llibre del Consolat de Mar* (Maritime Consulate Book). It was the first book of its kind and was translated and adopted as standard practice by the other Mediterranean powers, as well as by other Aragonese trading centres such as Palma and Valencia. By 1300 there were 126 consulates spread as far away as Flanders, Venice, Beirut and Constantinople. In these cities, Catalan traders competed with Venetians and Genoese for trade. The Catalan Jews were particularly active in the North African trade, exporting dried figs, rice, cheese, nuts and cloth to Africa and importing raw cotton, dyes and gold.

The commercial power of fourteenth century Barcelona is reflected in two buildings that survive to the present-day. The church of Santa Maria del Mar (Our Lady of the Sea) is the great public church of the Catalan Empire, where crews were blessed before setting out and gave thanks for safe returns. It is only because of later changes to the port area that its close links to the sea are not immediately apparent. The building of this Gothic masterpiece lasted from 1329 until 1390, a period which marks the high point of Barcelona's commercial success. A hundred yards along the sea-front is the Stock Exchange (*Llotja*). A rather fussy neo-classical exterior hides the lovely Gothic transactions hall which dates from 1392. The original building dates from about 1362 when it was established as a base for Catalan traders and consuls.

That Barcelona did not monopolise the maritime trade of the Kingdom of Aragon is evidenced by two more *llotjas*, one in Valencia, the other in Palma de Mallorca. The Palma exchange (*Sa Llotja*) dates from the first half of the fifteenth century, and as at Valencia has two parts: the exchange itself and the Consolat de Mar which was primarily concerned with maritime regulations. The latter is now the seat of the Balearic Islands government. The Valencian *Llotja* is a UNESCO world heritage site and arguably one of the pinnacles of European late Gothic architecture. Its building towards the end of the fifteenth century marks out that century as the 'Valencian century' and it is extraordinary to find so splendid a building devoted to such practical ends. The Consolat de Mar building dates from the first half of the sixteenth century but retains the Gothic style. The trading hall copies the spiral columns branching straight into the vaulting from its Palma model, but the whole is altogether richer and more elaborate. The tower that stands between the two parts of the building was used as a prison for traders who cheated customers or otherwise behaved scandalously. In later years the building was used as a silk exchange which explains its local name of *La Llotja de la Seda.*

The second Catalan empire represents the period in the nineteenth century when Catalans grew wealthy on trade with the remaining Spanish colonies in Cuba, Philippines and Puerto Rico. In the previous century, the loss of local rights in Valencia (from 1707) and Catalonia (from 1714) through the *Nova Planta* decrees had been felt as a grievous loss. The future Bourbon King and great central-izer Philip V had visited Barcelona in 1702, during the war to decide whether Spain should have a Hapsburg or Bourbon monarch. He had given assurances of

Barcelona's status as a free port with some participation in the American trade, and made encouraging noises about Catalan traditions and autonomy, even mentioning Valencia and the Balearics. But the Catalans refused to believe him and stuck to their preferred Hapsburg candidate to the bitter end of the Barcelona siege and capitulation of 1714.

However, political setbacks did not halt the startling economic development of Catalonia in particular. There was large-scale planting of vines and the growth of the wine and spirits industry, while the Royal Commercial Junta, established in Barcelona in 1758, encouraged the growth of a textile industry that included two thousand factories by the end of the century. Charles III called the Spanish parliament (the *Cortes*) into session. While he refused to consider the political complaints made by delegates from Aragon, Catalonia, Valencia and Mallorca, he did make a key concession in 1778, opening trade with the colonies in America to all ports, rather than just the Andalusian ports of Cadiz and Seville. This had little immediate effect, as the rise of revolutionary France and of Napoleon enveloped Europe in war, one of the by-products of which was that most of the American colonies became independent states under the watchful eye of the USA which now regarded the whole of the Americas as their sphere of influence.

The exceptions were Puerto Rico and Cuba, which remained Spanish colonies until 1898, and it was here that Catalan commercial efforts were centred. As part of Spain, Catalonia discovered possibilities previously denied to them, especially since most of Spain remained backward and rural, dominated by absentee landlords and inefficient agriculture. While merchants from Valencia, Alicante and Palma were also involved in trade with America, Barcelona was the dominant partner, providing the necessary capital and credits for commerce. The impact of colonial contacts reached outwards to quite small communities. At Vilanova i La Geltrú, south of Sitges, 1200 local people went to Cuba to make their fortunes in the first sixty years of the nineteenth century. Between 1803 and 1817, 24% of all the Catalans who arrived in Cuba came from this one town. Some returned to make major contributions to the development of their home town. Francesc Gumà i Ferran worked as a merchant and financier in Cuba and back home set up the local bank, financed a palatial railway station and established the local paper, now the *Diari de Vilanova*. Music travelled too, and Cuban *habaneres* are still played and sung at festival time all along the Catalan and Valencian coasts.

In Barcelona itself, the porticoed neo-classical block called the Porxos d'en Xifré opposite the Stock Exchange was built for Josep Xifré who had made his fortune exporting sugar grown on slave estates in Cuba to the United States of America. Returning to Barcelona in 1831 he rapidly diversified into banking and property, and became the largest property owner in town. The arcades are decorated with images of the sources of the wealth of the Caribbean: slaves, bananas and coffee especially. Amid the noise and fumes of this part of town, it is all too easy to miss the symbolism. Miquel Biada traded guns in Venezuela where they were used to exterminate troublesome Indian tribes, set up the first steam-driven cloth mill in his home town of Mataró, and built Spain's first railway — from Mataró to Barcelona — opened in 1848. The textile empire of the Güell family was based on America too. Joan Güell, father of Gaudí's patron Eusebi Güell, began his working life in a textile factory in Havana, Cuba. And after various travels and adventures, Güell established a cloth factory in the Barcelona suburb of Sants. While Valencia traded with the colonies (especially exporting wine), its economy remained more based on agriculture and less integrated into colonial markets.

5. Population movement in the twentieth and twenty-first centuries

In the contemporary European world, migration is a contradictory phenomenon, at once acknowledged as a consequence of globalisation, but equally the source of enormous social dislocation and controversy. For Catalonia, twentieth century migration involved the arrival of very large numbers of Castilian-speaking migrant workers from rural areas such as Andalusia and Galicia to work in factories. This in turn changed the linguistic character of Catalonia, and especially the Barcelona region, as we shall explore further in chapter 6. Potential conflict was exploited first by Franco in his efforts to eradicate all forms of Catalan expression, and more recently by the Popular Party (the ruling conservative party in Madrid at the time of writing) which has had considerable success in pulling over support by the Castilian-speaking working class from their traditional socialist allegiance.

During the Franquist period, Barcelona was crowded in on all sides by the shanty towns on the hills above, including Montjuïc, where migrant workers and their families lived in tumbledown shacks with little in the way of services such as water and sewage, let alone street lighting, pavements and schools for their children. Manuel Vázquez Montalbán has recorded this period in a very evocative way in his *Barcelonas*, and later recorded in his Pepe Carvalho novel *Southern Seas* the extent to which the rebuilding of these shanty towns as vast working-class high-rise estates perpetuated the separateness and alienation of these peripheral areas. Valencian-born Francesc Candel had reported on the lives of the shanty-town people in his 1964 book *Els Altres Catalans* (The Other Catalans), ironically one of the few Catalan best-sellers of the Franco period. Montalbán comments that Candel observed how previous pre-Civil War waves of Andalusian immigrants had been Catalanised by contact with the organised working class through trade unions and political parties, whereas these new immigrants from the south tended to live in ghettoes and had little contact with Catalans. Or for that matter with someone like myself when I lived and worked in Barcelona in the late 1960s. Now of course Barcelona is a great European city, visited each year by millions of people for reasons of business and pleasure. But the consequences of those years of uncontrolled migration into its slums still remain.

In areas such as the Costa Brava, Costa Blanca and the Balearics, the main engine of migration has been tourism. Jobs were created for locals, but also attracted many migrants from other parts of Spain. Many were young and some returned home after a season or two, but large numbers remained, again affecting the social and linguistic mix in Greater Catalonia. As the century drew to a close, two other groups of migrants have proved problematic, though for very different reasons. Firstly people from other European countries, especially older, retired people, have been attracted by the prospect of a year-round sunshine holiday world. They have settled in the holiday resorts themselves, especially down the Valencian coast and on the islands, but also in specially built 'urbanisations' in inland areas of the Valencian Community with associated swimming-pools and golf-courses which have made great environmental demands in one of Spain's driest corners. Some have become enthusiastic supporters of the culture and language of their new homes, but others remain confused about the identity of their new homes (Spain? Not Spain? Home? Not Home?) and their own place in that society. The bursting of the housing bubble in 2008 means that in addition to completed communities, it is also possible to see the half-built skeletons of abandoned projects. It is all rather confusing.

The second group of recent arrivals are migrant workers from poor countries in Asia, Africa and Latin America who were attracted to Spain and its booming economy at the end of the twentieth century. As in other parts of Europe, this has produced social and cultural conflicts and pressures on educational and health facilities, as well as new opportunities for cultural sharing. Arguably the Latin Americans, first-language speakers of Castilian Spanish, have fared rather better than others, especially Moroccans and North Africans stigmatised as 'Moors' in reference to the Muslim inhabitants of medieval Spain and subject to increasing Islamophobia as a result of jihadist terrorism around the world, including the Madrid train bombings of 2004. *El peaje de la vida* (The Toll of Life), by Sami Naïr and Juan Goytisolo is a moving account of the subject, unfortunately not yet available in English. In addition to a historical survey, they also place migration and conflict about migration within the context of the gross disparities of life-chances between the countries bordering the Mediterranean. There is surplus population and religious and political turmoil in North Africa and the Middle East, while Europe is identified as a land of opportunity, jobs and money, a view increasingly hard to either substantiate or dispel in recent years.

Migrants are trafficked into Europe, and many have died en route. Following the mass drownings in two accidents to heavily laden migrant boats off the Italian island of Lampedusa in October 2013, a special task force set up by the Italian government was responsible for saving over 100,000 lives. It is likely that in the future this work will concentrate on excluding would-be migrants rather than on saving them. In the long term, as will be explained in the final chapter of this book, only an international agreement on Mediterranean development can prevent further disasters. There is little doubt that the extent of illegal work in Spain (i.e. the employment of undocumented migrant workers) has exacerbated the problems associated with migration. Sami Naïr also questions whether the silence, the forgetting, of contemporary Spain does not include a forgetfulness of the years of dictatorship when Spanish people themselves were migrants, forced to flee to other European countries and to Latin America by political oppression, and by the oppression of poverty, the most persistent and debilitating oppression of all.

Finally, it is obvious that because of the history of these lands bordering the Mediterranean Sea, issues about migration and how to treat migrant workers become hopelessly confused with issues of history. In recent years, both the Spanish and Portuguese governments have offered automatic nationality to descendants of Sephardic Jews forced into exile in 1492. While it is unlikely that more than a few will take up this offer, it has provoked requests by the descendants of Spanish Moriscos exiled at the beginning of the seventeenth century for similar consideration. History has this way of coming back to haunt us, whether it is the activities of the Inquisition or the dream of *convivència*.

Chapter 4
Turbulent Times: Revolting People

There's no doubt that people mean others — and each one of us

1. A history of revolt 1400–1715

No country on earth has a history that is free of dissent and revolt. This is as true for the peoples of Greater Catalonia as of any other part of the world. The previous chapter was concerned mainly with the events leading up to forced conversions and expulsions of Jewish and Muslim populations of the area. It was certainly not the case that everything else in the Catalan, Valencian and Balearic gardens was rosy. In this chapter we shall be looking at conflict within the Christian communities and the impact this had on events in the region, beginning with the so-called Catalan Civil War of the fifteenth century and taking the story through to the loss of local rights in 1707/14. The subject of the Spanish Civil War, in retrospect a trialling ground or prelude to the wider global conflict of 1939–1945, will be dealt with in chapter 5, while in this chapter we shall jump to the issue of Catalan independence and explore a little what is pushing this agenda forward and why these calls have met with little support from the Valencians and the islanders. In doing so we shall suggest a number of approaches to consciousness of place in the world: class, local, national and global.

In the mid-fourteenth century, most of Europe was hit by the Black Death. This reduced populations and spread panic and fear. Because of the high death-rate, those workers who survived were able to demand higher wages, leading to conflicts between landlords, tenants and farm labourers and, in the towns, an increasing importance of the guilds in determining issues such as entry to trades and wage-rates. However, the Black Death was not a single event, or one that affected every society uniformly. In the Eastern Mediterranean, bubonic plague remained endemic until the nineteenth century. For reasons that are not altogether clear, Catalonia was especially badly affected by plague, losing probably half of its population between 1350 and 1500. This is in stark contrast to Valencia, which enjoyed in the fifteenth century the peak of its economic and artistic success.

The King of Aragon for most of the first half of the fifteenth century was Alfons the Magnanimous. It is more difficult to allocate him a number because of the complex affairs of the Aragonese crown: he was Alfons V as King of Aragon, Alfons IV as Count of Barcelona, Alfons III of Valencia, Alfons II of Mallorca and Alfons I of Naples from 1442 until his death in 1458. The Italian connection is significant. As King of Naples, Alfons ruled over one of the great Renaissance courts of Europe. He counted among his employees the artist Pisanello who designed the portrait medal of Alfons' lieutenant Iñigo d'Avalos which gives a vivid impression of the imperial ambitions of the Catalans. The other side of the medal shows the globe, with stars, land and sea, a symbol of imperial conquest. But Barcelona was not Rome, and never had been. Through Naples, great art and artistic ideas flowed west, especially to Valencia, but with Alfons an absentee king, the people of Catalonia became restless. Alfons earned his title the Magnanimous by favouring for a time the interests of peasants against landlords. He abolished the *remences* (taxes on peasants which maintained them in a state of serfdom) in 1455, and allowed the peasants to set up a guild to protect their interests, but was forced by the nobles and the church to reverse his policy the following year. The peasant agitators took the name *remences* from the taxes for which they were liable. The son of Alfons who ruled as Joan II (John II) did not show anything like the fleetness of political reflex of his father, and in 1462 war broke out between king and nobles with peasant uprisings as a backdrop. It was the worst of all possible worlds. In the towns artisans fought merchants; in the countryside peasants fought landowners, especially in the foothills of the Pyrenees beyond Gerona. Sporadic fighting continued until 1472. The country had been brought to its knees and it was still not clear who had won.

Joan II looked for support across the border in Castile, but in order to secure support from Castile, which was being courted by the Catalan nobles, he married his son Ferdinand in 1469 to the Castilian princess Isabella. When the *remences* revolted again in 1485, Ferdinand stepped in very quickly to mediate between peasants and lords, to abolish the worst abuses, and to allow a cash sum to be paid for emancipation from serfdom. This event is commemorated by a decorative plaque in the monastery at Amer, just west of Gerona, set up in 1985 to celebrate the 400th anniversary. As Ferdinand and Isabella, they were to rule as the 'Catholic Monarchs' and set Spain off in a new direction which had nothing to do with the Mediterranean and from which Catalans, Valencians and islanders were to be firmly excluded. There was more trouble ahead.

By 1500, Catalonia had been pacified, and the focus of trouble moved further south. The revolt of the *Germanies* in Valencia (1519–1523) and Mallorca (1521–1523) like that of the *Comuneros* in Castile (1520–1522), has been largely ignored by English language writers: such episodes do not fit into easily recognised narratives of Spanish history. Both have a strong whiff of class conflict, both have strong elements of local or peripheral revolt against centralised power. Added to this, the actions in Valencia acquired an unpleasant tinge of Islamophobia which fed into the final collapse of the notion of *convivència* in Greater Catalonia. The sixteenth century opened badly in Valencia. There were outbreaks of plague in 1508 and 1509, and serious floods in 1517. There was serious concern about whether the new unified crown of Aragon-Castile, with its increasing orientation towards Europe and America, would continue to recognise the *furs* — the collection of local rights built up over the years by city councils and by the Valencian Generalitat (the representative assembly which shared some of the royal authority). These rights were of special importance in urban areas, where they placed considerable powers in the hands of the guilds, and were used as a brake on the power of the nobility. In so far as the *Germanies* had an ideology, it was a confused one. They were pro-monarchist, seeing royal power as defending local rights against the nobility, a theme which links *Germanies* and *Comuneros* and is also one of the themes of Spanish Golden Age drama, especially in plays such as Lope de Vega's *Fuenteovejuna*. Their struggle was given a certain legitimacy by the decision of King Charles I (Carlos I) to allow the *Germanies* to arm themselves against the threat of Ottoman pirates. But there is also the inspiration of the Italian city-states, the idea of local self-government.

The revolt was already in its third year when in the summer of 1521 the rebels turned on the Valencian Mudejars as an enemy, leading to attacks on Muslim property, murders, the saying of masses in mosques, and forced conversions. Matthew Carr in his otherwise excellent book *Blood and Faith: the Purging of Muslim Spain* includes a chapter on the Muslims of Valencia but tends to elide the social and economic complaints of the Valencian guildsmen with anti-Muslim actions which came several years into the revolt. Meyerson suggests that the important role in agriculture played by the Mudejars and their relative willingness to accept their

94

position as serfs of the great barons, were contributory factors. They farmed land owned by the nobles and paid rents and taxes to them. In addition they often served in the armies raised by the nobles. Both sets of circumstances meant they became identified with the cause of the nobility. On the other hand, Christians and Muslims worked side-by-side in the craft guilds, and the fact that the *Germanies* received less support in the inland territory around Morella (the Ports de Morella), where the Muslim population was relatively low, may well have reasons other than the small number of Muslims in that area.

Violence against the Mudejars was especially fierce in Xativa, where several hundred were dragged from the Muslim quarter to the cathedral and given the choice of baptism or death. Another centre of murder and forced baptism was Gandia where the local duke had recruited large numbers of Muslim labourers from his sugar plantations to fight against the *Germanies*. The revolt ended in defeat for the rebels and the decimation of both the Valencian countryside and the Mudejar population. By 1525 the King/Emperor Charles, with the support of the Inquisition was able to declare that all Muslims who had not yet been baptised must convert or leave. There was some resistance, notably the siege of Muslims at Benaguacil, inland from Valencia City, and further north in the Espadán Mountains (Serra d'Espadà), where rebels were eventually defeated by German mercenaries. Relative order was re-established in Valencia by Germaine de Foix, second wife of King Ferdinand, who was appointed as regent. She made peace with the *Germanies* and instigated the progressive Castilianisation of Valencian society, or at least its upper classes. The Mudejars who remained acquired the new name and status of Moriscos. As Carr summarises the outcome: 'By the end of 1526, the would-be World Emperor [Charles I] had managed to pull off the seemingly impossible task of eradicating the last outpost of Islam from Spain, while simultaneously retaining the labour force on whom the prosperity of his Aragonese kingdoms [sic] depended.'

Some aspects of the *Germanies* revolt in Valencia in both urban and rural settings are comparable to the civil war fought in Catalonia in the previous century, but it was noticeable that the *Germanies* revolt did not receive support from the Catalans. However, events in Valencia inspired revolt on the island of Mallorca. Following the imprisonment of a number of guild members on the island, a Council of Thirteen, led by Joan Crespí, was established, in direct imitation of a similar council in Valencia. The use of the number thirteen is significant: it represents a strain of mystical, almost millenarian sentiment in these revolts, the number standing for Christ and the twelve apostles. The rebels gained control of Palma, slaughtered many of the nobles at Bellver Castle and ruled the island for nearly two years. In August 1522 the King/Emperor Charles sent 800 men to restore order and this was achieved by the following spring. Two hundred of the island's *agermanats* were executed. Crespí himself was already dead, murdered in prison by a more radical faction of the movement led by Joanot Colom.

One third of the way into the sixteenth century, local rights were hanging by a thread throughout the lands that had once been the Kingdom of Aragon. The most surprising thing is that the fragile thread retained at least some of its historical strength for nearly another 200 years, before finally breaking in the events of 1707/14. Certainly the Catalans' sense of the thread was not sufficiently strong to provoke them into support for the guild revolts in Valencia and Mallorca. Throughout the country now known as Spain, rights had been replaced by royal prerogative, and where rights remained, it was best to keep quiet about them. This is not to say they were not a cause of concern for Spanish rulers. The Count Duke of Olivares, chief minister of Philip IV was especially exercised over this. The artist Velázquez painted his portrait in 1634, an equestrian portrait which suggests a man of action, although his main skills were in administration. His aim was nothing less than to establish throughout Spain a uniform system of laws and taxes that would fund Hapsburg interests throughout Europe. He also wanted soldiers to fight for the Catholic cause in the vastly expensive and vastly destructive Thirty Years War (1618–1648). Catalonia was required to raise 16,000 men, and in addition to this drain on its labour force, also required to lodge and feed foreign troops and their horses during outbreaks of war with France in 1622 and again in 1635. When Olivares wrote in 1640, 'Really, the Catalans ought to see more of the world than Catalonia', there is a curious reverse echo of modern sentiments in Spain that suggest the Catalans are concerned with their own narrow interests at the expense of the 'bigger picture', whatever that may be!

Two significant Catalan institutions had survived incorporation into the new Spain: the Council of One Hundred which had authority in Barcelona, and the Catalan Generalitat which retained some power across the territory. Both were determined to pursue their own 'narrow interests' rather than the interests of the Hapsburg Empire. In 1640 the authorities imprisoned several members of the Council of One Hundred, together with Pau Claris, a priest who was also President of the Generalitat. In response 1,500 peasants left the harvest fields, entered Barcelona and freed the prisoners. In doing so they provided Catalonia with its national anthem *Els Segadors* (The Reapers). The link between rural peasants and urban guildsmen was something of a replay of the civil war of two centuries before, but this time directed at an external enemy — the Hapsburg monarchy. Just as the Catalans had chosen to look the other way in 1520, so the Valencians and islanders now chose to ignore events in Catalonia. If there is mistrust between the component parts of Greater Catalonia, it has good historical precedents.

The only place to look for support was France, and under Pau Claris, the Generalitat pronounced Louis XIII as king of Catalonia. A French army marched in and defeated the Hapsburg army at Montjuïc, but most of the French army departed in 1648 at the conclusion of the Thirty Years War, leaving the Catalans alone. After a year's siege, Barcelona surrendered in 1652. Apart from the disgrace of Olivares (he became mentally ill and died in 1645), little had been won, and territory lost. Under the terms of the Treaty of the Pyrenees in 1659, the French took North Catalonia — the Catalan counties of Rosselló (Roussillon), Conflent, Vallespir, Capcir and the upper half of the Cerdanya (Alt Cerdanya). This redrawing of the map reduced the population of Catalonia by one fifth. But someone in a palace somewhere did not get it quite right. And the pretty little town of Llívia remains to this day stranded, an outpost of Spain among the green fields of France, or just another town in Catalonia, depending on your point of view.

Contemporary Catalans often look to Portugal for inspiration: if Portugal has managed to remain an independent country, then why not Catalonia? Unfortunately history does not take account of such ideas of fair play. Portugal had not been involved in the shotgun marriage of Castile and Aragon and had developed its own empire in Africa, Brazil and Asia. Philip II had become joint king of both Spain and Portugal in 1580 after a disputed succession problem, but the Portuguese never settled under Spanish rule in general, and the rule of Olivares in particular. In Brazil, Portuguese explorers and settlers spread through the Amazon basin on the pretext of being temporarily 'Spanish', where previously they had been restricted to the Atlantic seaboard. With the support of English and French troops, they declared independence in 1640 under King John IV, an independence finally recognised by the Spanish in 1668.

Rather remarkably, Catalan institutions south of the new border with France remained intact after 1659 and Hapsburg monarchs continued to swear unenthusiastically to respect Catalan rights. The next outbreak of trouble involved all the territories of Greater Catalonia, with the exception of North Catalonia, now firmly in French hands and defended by Vauban's vast new fortress at Mont Lluís. The War of the Spanish Succession was characterised by strange and shifting alliances and, not for the first time, Catalans, Valencians and Mallorcans found themselves on the losing side of history. The last Spanish Hapsburg King-Emperor, Charles II, had died in 1700 without an heir, a state of affairs that threatened to unbalance the uneasy peace of Europe. The two main candidates for the job were the Archduke Charles of Austria (Hapsburg) and Philip of Anjou (Bourbon). It was Philip who made the initial running, and was crowned as Philip V. This alliance of two of Europe's major powers was anathema to Austria, England and Holland. So what had begun as a local Spanish affair rapidly escalated into all-out European war.

The Catalans, betrayed by their French allies fifty years before, had been treated perhaps rather better than they deserved by the Hapsburgs, and supported the Austrian candidate, as did Valencia and Mallorca. Philip V did at least visit Barcelona in 1702, but by offering the Catalans everything they might wish for (respect for local rights, participation in the Americas trade) he overplayed his hand. It was too good to be true and certainly too good to believe. In 1703, Archduke Charles, now playing catch-up, was crowned in Vienna as Charles III of Castile, but also of Aragon and Catalonia. In 1705, with the war going well for the Hapsburgs, the Aragonese territories declared publicly for Charles. The Portuguese were drawn into the alliance, which meant that now the English navy had a secure naval bases at Lisbon, a situation later improved still further with the capture of Gibraltar. Consequently, the English fleet was now able to operate in the Mediterranean and Bourbon Spain was under attack from both east and west. Even so, Charles did not receive the amount of support he had expected in Spain. By 1707, Valencia and Saragossa had both been recaptured by the Bourbon forces, and Philip V moved immediately to abolish local rights — the *furs* of Valencia and the *fueros* of Aragon. Those areas still supporting the Hapsburgs were the Catalan lands east of the River Segre and north of the River Ebro.

The peace conference that met at Utrecht in 1712 was concerned with the wider picture, not just the balance of power in Europe but also colonial issues in America and the West Indies. From an English point of view, Catalonia was just another piece on the chess-board of international relations, and in 1713 the English made their own separate peace, which gave them not only the naval base of Gibraltar, but also the island of Menorca with its fine deep-water harbour at Mahon. Perfidious Albion had had a good war. Most of the powers except Austria had now settled, and in 1714 Charles became, rather to his own surprise, Charles VI of the Holy Roman Empire, a job he found more appealing than Charles III of the unruly Spanish. The English and the Dutch, as alarmed by too close an alliance between Austria and Spain as they had been by too close an alliance between France and Spain, were now quite sure that Charles must be kept permanently out of Spain. The Catalans were left on their own, and had only their own heroism by which to remember a disastrous war. The Bourbons laid siege to Barcelona. People starved, religious fanaticism ruled, and Barcelona, led by its Council of One Hundred, did not surrender. On 11 September 1714, the Bourbons entered Barcelona. As almost a footnote to this tragic episode, Mallorca held out for a further nine months before it surrendered to the Bourbons in July 1715.

Even fifty years ago, the 11 September was considered to be more a cause for mourning than celebration in Catalonia. It was St George's Day which saw the most fervent demonstrations of loyalty to the Catalan cause, including the odd battle with Franco's police and ritual smashing of shop windows. Now the 11 September (*La Diada*) has become the most public focus of demands for independence. It is interesting and instructive here to compare what has happened in the Valencian Community in relation to a national day. There are supporters of April 25, date of the defeat of the Hapsburg forces at the battle of Almansa in 1707, leading directly to the abolition of Valencian rights, the equivalent of Catalan celebrations of 11 September. Others prefer October 9, date of James I's triumphal entry into Valencia City in 1238, while yet others prefer Hispanic (or Columbus) Day, October 12, although this became greatly devalued in Spain by the propaganda organised around that day by the Franco regime and its curiously inappropriate slogan 'Spain — One, Great and Free'.

An article by Enric and Rafael Castelló has analysed participation on such days over the past 25 years. October 12 receives little support in Valencia except from fringe right-wing organisations, and is best reflected in Spanish media such as the main television channel. October 9 tends to be a civic event with a procession from Valencia Town Hall to the statue of James I via the cathedral where a Te Deum is sung. April 25 is the date that has attracted most popular participation. As the Castelló brothers report: 'The April 25th festival had been transformed into the *Dia de les Corts Valencians* (Day of the Valencian Parliament). The motive behind this celebration is to commemorate the loss of political autonomy and to call for its restitution in democratic times.' But in truth, neither October 9 nor April 25 has succeeded in establishing itself as a true National Day, support and participation waxing and waning with the electoral cycle. In that sense it reflects the complex issue of national identity in the Valencian Community, with minorities identifying themselves as 'more Spanish than Valencian' and 'more Valencian than Spanish', but a good half the population happy to sit on the fence and accept both national identities.

101

2. The grace of democracy, 1976–

As we have seen, the existence of Portugal as a nation state is one accident of history: the non-existence of Greater Catalonia as a nation state is another. As Burns neatly summed it up: 'Spanish unity was not a destiny but an accident.' Two features of the contemporary scene in Greater Catalonia call immediate attention. Firstly the growing clamour for independence in Catalonia, and secondly the low level of political support in the other areas — Valencian Community, Balearic Islands and North Catalonia — for either claims of independence at a local level or for a *Països Catalans* (Greater Catalonia) outcome.

In reaching an evaluation of the Catalan 'Road to Independence' it helps to consider something of the politics of the democratic post-Franquist Generalitat, the Catalan autonomous government. From the first democratic elections in 1980 until his retirement in 2003, the Generalitat was run by its President Jordi Pujol, 'the politician who never lost an election.' Imprisoned under Franco, a successful entrepreneur devoted to the cause of building up the Catalan economy, he was a careful, astute politician who managed to proceed with caution and cunning to making sure that Catalan autonomy always had a strong nationalist turn, while avoiding overblown nationalist language. The exact nature of that nationalist turn — ethnic or civil? — has been much debated. Pujol claimed that everyone who lived in Catalonia was to be considered as a Catalan, but he also oversaw the policy known as 'linguistic normalisation' by which Catalan replaced Castilian as the language of street signs, advertising and (most crucially) of education. It came as rather a shock when it was revealed in 2014 that Pujol was being investigated for non-payment of taxes and squirrelling away considerable amounts of money in foreign bank accounts.

Pujol's electoral success was aided by a number of factors. Elections to the Generalitat are run on a differential basis in the four provinces making up the autonomous territory. Votes are weighted to ensure that rural voters in Lerida, Tarragona and Gerona are not swamped by the heavily urbanised and industrialised province of Barcelona. For example, in the 2003 election, there was one seat per 11,000 voters in Lerida, but in Barcelona it was one seat per 28,000 electors. Even so, 85 of the 135 seats in the Generalitat are allocated to Barcelona province.

In the UK we are rather used to electors maintaining their preference in local and national elections. In Catalonia there is a strong tendency towards variation, and the impact is exacerbated by the broadly proportional methods used to assess election outcomes. Thus working-class people whose families originated outside Catalonia, often the poor rural south, tended to abstain in Catalan elections, which were seen as the business of the Catalans themselves. This reduced the socialist vote, while other voters who identified with the socialist cause at a Spanish level, expressed their Catalan sense of identity by voting for Pujol's CiU party at Catalan elections. By contrast, socialist votes ensured that the mayor of Barcelona was usually a socialist, with Barcelona identity taking precedence over Catalan identity. To this complicated state of affairs must be added the absence until the early part of the present century of a convincing 'independentist' party. ERC (Catalan Republican Left) had been the party of power during the Second Republic and the Civil War, but before 2000 tended to attract a rather incoherent protest vote. Its potential trump card has always been Lluís Companys, the President of the wartime Generalitat, returned to Barcelona in 1940 by the Nazis, and summarily executed at Montjuïc. Every cause needs a martyr.

In the present century, both the PSC (Catalan Socialist Party, allied to the Spanish socialist party PSOE) and ERC have developed more coherent political programmes.

Pasqual Maragall, socialist president of the Generalitat (2003–2006), had come to prominence as Mayor of Barcelona at the time of the Barcelona Olympic Games in 1992. He proved adept at promoting Barcelona as a safe haven for incoming capital, often expressed in large-scale building works such as the redesigned port area and the installations for the Games themselves. At the same time, he received working-class support for the extensive urban improvements (parks, urban open spaces, public squares and so on) throughout the city, including the peripheral working-class estates previously ignored by public policy. Maragall was the grandson of one of Catalonia's greatest national poets, Joan Maragall, and his overall aim seems to have been to move Spain towards a more federalist system of government.

What happened next was a tragedy for Catalonia and, in the light of subsequent events, very possibly for Spain itself. Maragall had worked hard to reform and expand the Catalan statute of autonomy (the *Estatut*) and achieved a reasonable compromise that managed to include both the Catalans' preferred version of Catalonia as a nation, and the preferred Spanish version of a nationality, whatever that might mean. The revised *Estatut* was put to a referendum and received overwhelming support. Maragall passed over the presidency in 2006 to José Montilla, the son of Andalusian immigrants and the first non-Catalan to be president of the Generalitat. Within a year, Maragall had been diagnosed with Alzheimer's and used his remaining energies to set up a foundation dedicated to searching for a cure for that crippling disease. Meanwhile, the conservative Popular Party used their influence in the Constitutional Court to overturn both that part of the *Estatut* which referred to a nation, and specific clauses which awarded increased 'tax and spend' powers to the Generalitat, leading to a growth of nationalist sentiment in Catalonia which initially favoured CiU but later a reinvigorated ERC.

The ERC has become a prominent part of the Catalan government scene, first as part of the 'tripartite' government with the socialists and greens, and more recently in coalition with CiU itself. In 2010 CiU fell just short of an overall majority but was able to govern with tacit support from the conservative Popular Party. However, this situation changed dramatically in 2012 in the wake of deepening Catalan scepticism about the ability of the Madrid government to deal with the ongoing crisis in the Spanish economy and banking system, or to respond effectively to growing grass-roots demands for greater autonomy, even independence for Catalonia. In the years since the banking crisis of 2008 and the subsequent economic crisis, there has been a progressive weakening in the links between public concerns and the political parties. There was a deep sense that neither the economy nor the state was capable any longer of delivering the social goods that citizens required.

By 2011, 1-in-5 of the working-age population of Spain were unemployed and youth unemployment had reached nearly 50%. Working at a community level, but making considerable use of digital media, people came together in a movement variously described as the 15-M (the day chosen for mass demonstrations in Spanish cities, including Greater Catalonia, was 15 May 2011) the Indignants and Take the Square. In Barcelona and Madrid, protesters formed camps in the main city squares (Puerta del Sol in Madrid, Plaça Catalunya in Barcelona). May 22 was the day of the Spanish General Election, and despite a resounding victory for the conservative People's Party, a record number of spoilt ballot papers reflected the concern that conventional politics no longer represented voters' real concerns. On May 27 police were sent in to clear the Barcelona camp ahead of the Champions' League football final to be played in the city the following day. Sporadic outbreaks of street protests continued throughout 2011 and into 2012.

While at one level, the protests linked citizens, especially young people, in all parts of Spain, the protests in Catalonia became very closely linked to the demands for greater political autonomy, bringing political authority, now seen as remote and irrelevant, closer to people's everyday and local concerns. There are many memories of the 1970s in the events of 2012: in the 1970s, Catalan people had come together in massive demonstrations in support of Catalan autonomy, now they were coming together to express their concern that the limited autonomy allowed under the Estatut was no longer acceptable. Whereas the demonstrations of the 1970s had been orchestrated by the Catalan Assembly, in which political parties played a major role, the demonstration on 11 September 2012 was organised by the new Catalan National Assembly (ANC in Catalan and Castilian), a non-party political organisation.

Kathryn Crameri's 2014 book, *'Goodbye Spain?' The Question of Independence for Catalonia* charts the rise of citizen movements in Catalonia. Òmnium Cultural was founded in 1961 and promotes cultural activities, Plataforma per la Llengua (Platform for the Language, 1993) is concerned above all with the Catalan language. The ANC, founded in 2012, has as its president Carme Forcadell, a Catalan linguist and teacher, previously a founder member of the Plataforma, and also a member of Òmnium Cultural, and this cross-membership is very common. The strength of the ANC is undoubtedly in its sophisticated grassroots organisation and related use of social media, which makes it possible to organise massive events such as those of recent years. It also, ironically, benefits from the very divisive nature of Catalan politics, since it would be very difficult to describe it as a front organisation for any one party. ANC presents people with a choice (albeit a deceptively simple choice!) of independence or continuing Spanish hegemony. As we saw in the Scottish referendum, it was only in the final weeks that there was any detailed discussions of what 'independence' actually means, and the way it might be actualised, that is, turned from a paper notion to a series of specific changes happening in real time in a real world. For example, the 'Dret de Decidir' (Right to Decide) is a major slogan used by pro-independence campaigners, but rather leaves out of the equation the subject-matter of the decision-making and the policies an independent Catalonia might pursue.

As part of the general social unrest in Catalonia, attitudes to national identity have shifted considerably. A comparison by Luis Moreno of the Spanish National Research Council (CSIC) of attitudes in 1985 and 2013 shows an increase from 9% to 31% in those identifying themselves as exclusively Catalan, while adding in those who feel more Catalan than Spanish produces a figure well over 50%. This begins to make sense of opinion poll findings that show support for independence relatively steady over the period 2012-14 at about 45-50%, since these attitude changes reflect not just the increasing self-confidence of Catalans in their ability to run a successful autonomous regime, but the determined opposition of the Spanish state to any extension of that autonomy.

The actual size of the massive ANC-led demonstration in 2012 is disputed (this is common to all large-scale demonstrations, but especially those in Spain!) with organisers claiming two million supporters on the streets, and press and police offering more modest figures in the region of half a million. Significantly, whereas in the great public shows of support for autonomy of the 1970s, demonstrators waved the Catalan flag (the *senyera*), in 2012 they had added a new form of the flag with a white star on a blue background at the base of the flag (the *estelada*) signifying support for independence. The replacement of one banner by another intensified in the following years. On 11 September 2013, demonstrators linked hands through the country in a chain intended to stretch from the French border to the Valencian Community. In 2014 they formed a giant V (for victory) along the main avenues of Barcelona reflecting the significance of the independence referendum called on 9 November 2014 and declared illegal by the constitutional court.

To return to the events of 2012, the political classes in Catalonia were now faced with a dilemma. The ruling party (CiU) was a nationalist party that had never expressed itself in support of independence. However, the President, Artur Mas, following a meeting with the ANC leaders, moved swiftly to call snap elections in November 2012. Mas had been involved in failed talks with the Spanish president, Mariano Rajoy, concerning the so-called 'fiscal deficit'. This is a complicated business, but in summary Catalonia pays more into Spanish coffers than it receives back in the value of services and grants to run the Generalitat, a situation which in some ways is common sense, given that Catalonia is traditionally the richest area of Spain, but also conceals a deep-seated Catalan conviction about the incompetence, inefficiency and corruption that lie at the heart of the Spanish government. The outcome of the election was not quite what President Mas had hoped for. Support for both major parties declined by nearly 10% compared with the previous election of 2010. Support for the independence-supporting ERC nearly doubled to 20%. The green-left grouping moved up to 10%, only just behind the socialists.

Coalition has always been a fact of life in Catalan politics, and ERC now entered into coalition with CiU to run the Generalitat. It was an uneasy partnership: a moderate nationalist party favouring a liberal economic policy, and a party favouring independence and critical of the full-blown economic crisis released by the forces of economic liberalism. While having ERC on board made it easier for CiU to appeal to nationalist sympathies within Catalan society, the presence of ERC in government made it doubly difficult for Mas to conduct any kind of meaningful negotiations with Madrid. Within a year the coalition partners had hammered out a plan for a referendum on 9 November 2014 with two questions:

1   'Do you want Catalonia to be a state?'

2   'If so, do you want Catalonia to be an independent
    state?'

Clearly the hope was to have a process comparable to the
Scotland referendum also planned for the autumn of
2014, in which regional and national governments would
commit themselves to both the referendum and to the
result, whatever that might be. However, this was a
grave miscalculation. Over the two years from 2012-2014,
opposition in Madrid to the referendum plans was not
only maintained but increased. The Madrid government
centred its case on the 1978 democratic constitution
which confirmed Spain as a unified nation, a state in
which autonomous regions held considerable powers, but
did not have the right to either join together or to challenge the essential unity of Spain itself. Even more
worryingly, right-wing commentators also emphasised
the role of the army as the defender of this essential unity
against any challenge. It was an ugly situation for any
democratic country to find itself in. A crucial vote took
place in the Spanish Parliament (the *Cortes*) in April
2014 refusing the transfer of powers to hold referendums
to the Generalitat. Consequently when the official call for
the referendum was put out in September 2014, the
Constitutional Court moved immediately to block the
procedure, holding out the prospect not only that politicians in the Catalan Generalitat would be breaking the
law but that any state employee taking part (for example
as poll clerks or returning officers) would also be
breaking the law. While this bitter opposition from
Madrid enhanced the nationalist credentials of Mas, he
was forced to back down over the planned referendum,
substituting only a 'consultation' that would be staffed by
volunteers, and based on the presentation of identity
cards rather than an electoral register.

It is difficult for outsiders to understand the attitude of
the Spanish government, especially so soon after the

referendum on Scottish independence organised jointly by the UK government and Scottish government, with both parties committed to the outcome. Prime Minister Rajoy's public statement on the day of the vote that what was happening was neither a referendum nor a consultation showed an alarming lack of knowledge of events in Catalonia, not to say sensitivity to opinion in the principality. Well over two million people voted, over one third of those registered to vote in Catalan elections. Of these, 80% voted 'Yes-Yes', in other words in support of the view of Catalonia as an independent nation, with a further 10% assenting to the notion of nation, but not linked to independence. While Rajoy was showing a complete disinterest, Pedro Sánchez, Secretary-General of the Spanish socialist party (PSOE) sped off to Barcelona the morning after the vote to consult with his Catalan comrades. No doubt top of the agenda was the project of a new federal constitution for Spain, but since such a change would require a two-thirds majority in the *Cortes*, plus approval in a referendum, it is a scenario which at present seems rather unlikely. Meanwhile opinion polls in Spain were showing both conservatives and socialists lagging behind the new community-based party Podemos.

Earlier in this chapter, we saw Catalans and Valencians both sitting on their hands while great events were taking place in their neighbours' back-yards (1520 in Valencia and Mallorca; 1640 in Catalonia). That has been rather what has happened in the case of the referendum/consultation. Official attitudes in both the Valencian Community and Balearic Islands, both governed until 2015 by the same conservative Popular Party, lined up against Catalonia, as might be expected. In both areas, nationalist sentiment was divided between two minorities, one of which favoured more extensive powers rather closer to home than pan-Catalanism, and another even smaller minority which still clung to the distant dream of a Greater Catalonia.

In Valencia, where the citizens' movement has been especially influential and the new Podemos party received considerable support at the 2014 European elections, political attention has been more closely linked to the extent of political corruption in Valencia, and a series of high-profile scandal in which even the Royal Family has become embroiled. These accusation involved Princess Cristina, sister of the new King Philip (Felipe VI). The high court in Palma de Mallorca determined at the end of 2014 that she must face trial on tax fraud charges, while dropping money-laundering charges. These charges relate to business activities by her husband, the ex-professional handball player Iñaki Urdangarín. He and fourteen others stand accused of embezzling large amounts of public money invested in the sports charity, the Nóos Institute, which organised a series of sporting events for the regional governments of the Balearic Islands and Valencia, events for which they stand accused of overcharging. Princess Cristina was a board member of Nóos when her husband was its president.

Many of the public scandals that have hit the Valencian Community in the past ten years have related to precisely the kind of high-profile projects that it was hoped would make Valencia a desirable location for business, tourism and sport. These projects have included hosting the America's Cup sailing race, the European motor-racing Grand Prix, and the building of an aquarium, opera house and new museums. Money was easy after Spain joined the euro, and politicians became used to receiving kick-backs from the awarding of contracts to their cronies. Remarkably, the party which has presided over so much corruption, the Popular Party, remained in power until the regional elections of 2015 in both Valencia and the Balearics. It is only since the rise of the Indignants movement and Podemos that there has been any sign that the people of Valencia have had enough of political corruption. The one issue that might have attracted support to the disgruntled Catalans has been the issue of the use the Valencian and Balearic versions of Catalan in education, which will be dealt with at some length in chapter 6, including the use of Catalan in North Catalonia.

In North Catalonia, there has been rather muted reaction to the Catalan independence issue, and it is clear that Catalanism is understood there in rather different ways to South Catalonia (a term used by Catalans in France to balance the use of the term North Catalonia). There has been growing interest in establishing exactly what the dual identity of being both French and Catalan actually means. In 2008 Perpignan was chosen as the Capital of Catalan Culture, which gave the city an opportunity to show off traditional Catalan culture as well as remembering under the theme of Peace some of the outstanding figures of North Catalonia. These included Oliba, abbot of Ripoll and of its northern dependency at Cuixà in the shadow of the Canigó (often described as the holy mountain of the Catalans), the Perpignan rabbi Al Meiri who promoted interfaith dialogue in a city with a distinguished Jewish past, and more recent figures such as Walter Benjamin the German-Jewish intellectual who died at Portbou fleeing the Nazis in 1940 and Pau Casals, cellist, democrat and Catalan nationalist, who inaugurated an annual summer music festival at Prades (Prada) in North Catalonia from 1950. He died in exile, having sworn never to return to Spain while Franco lived.

Although Catalanists north of the border value their language and culture, their Catalan flags and their bilingual street signs, they also know that Perpignan remains closely linked to Paris and the highly centralised French state. The arguments in support of independence in South Catalonia (the fiscal deficit, investment in infrastructure, the general hostility of the Madrid government) simply do not apply to North Catalonia. However, all this might change in the future in the unlikely event that France became a less centralised country. Already there are the first signs of this in the regional assembly of Languedoc-Roussillon, which ironically links together lands which were once very much part of early medieval Catalonia. It has adopted a new flag, moving away from the traditional Catalan red stripes on a yellow ground, and if it decided to adopt a new name which did away with the Catalan identity suggested by Roussillon, one of the historic Catalan counties of North Catalonia, this might lead to an increase in nationalist sentiment in North Catalonia.

During the Middle Ages, Greater Catalonia acted together as constituent parts of the Crown of Aragon. Once Aragon was absorbed into the new Spain of the Catholic Kings, history began to edge the territories apart. The *Germanies* revolts in Valencia and Mallorca in the sixteenth century, the Catalan revolts of the *remences* in the fifteenth century and again in the seventeenth century, these were separate episodes of revolt and opposition. Briefly at the beginning of the eighteenth century, the territories were allies in the pro-Hapsburg cause in the War of the Spanish Succession which led to the loss of all their traditional rights. In the nineteenth century, the small industrial town of Alcoy in the Valencian Community became an important international centre of anarchism, but in general the Valencian economy continued to be based on agriculture. There is no equivalent to the development of Barcelona as a centre of bitter class conflict between factory owners, state and police on one hand, and the organised working class — whether anarchist or socialist — on the other. It is this tradition of the *Rosa del Foc* (the Rose of Fire) which comes to mind so readily when one sees images of mass rallies in Barcelona for whatever cause.

The success of the independence movement in Catalonia in the past few years has been to channel discontent about corruption, unemployment, and the evils of globalism into one movement. As if somehow, an independent Catalonia could at one bound leap away from all the misery and suffering of the modern world. Put that way, it sounds almost comical. And yet as the poet Maria Mercè Marçal expressed it so succinctly, there is no doubt that the domination of one nation (Catalonia) by another (Spain) is part of the story of ongoing oppression:

> A l'atzar agraeixo tres dons: haver nascut dona,
> De clase baixa i nació oprimida.
> I el tèrbol atzar de ser tres voltes rebel.

> *(I am grateful to fate for three gifts: to have been born a woman / from the working-class and an oppressed nation. / And the uncertain fate of being three times a rebel.)*

What lies in store for Catalonia may be uncertain, but equally the same can be said for the rest of Greater Catalonia, the rest of Spain. We live in troubled, turbulent times.

Chapter 5
Silence and Memory

Often, in fact almost always, to remain silent is also to lie.

As a writer in Franquist Spain, Joan Fuster knew all about keeping silent. Or not, because the great triumph of Fuster against dictatorship and censorship was to allow for the intelligence of the reader to fill in the gaps between words. The very fact of writing in Catalan, and being published in Catalan, was itself an achievement. Others writing in Catalan had a filing-cabinet full of manuscripts by the time censorship began to relax in the late 1960s, early 1970s. By then it was very inefficient too. I remember getting involved in a tussle at the railway station in Portbou between two Dutch students and the border police. The police were trying to deny them entry on the basis of a vague similarity with a photo they were holding taken at an anti-Franquist demonstration somewhere in the south of France, and the clear crime of having books in their rucksack by Karl Marx. Quite calmly I explained that I was a teacher at the University of Barcelona (true) and that Karl Marx was now on the syllabus (he may have been). The young Dutchmen were allowed in but I ignored them politely all the way down to Barcelona. Just in case.

One of the many songs we used to sing on evenings out with the students was one by the Valencian singer Raimon, in those heady days one of the Left's political treasures. It was called 'Sobre la pau' (About peace):

De vegades la pau
Fa gust de mort.
Dels morts per sempre,
Dels que son no més silenci.
De vegades la pau
Fa gust de mort.

(There are times when peace / tastes of death. / Of people who have always been dead, / of people who are just silence. / There are times when peace / tastes of death)

The meaning is not apparent until one hears it sung in Raimon's gravelly, angry tones, until one think of the date (1967) and the celebrations of the Franquist regime in 1964 of 'Twenty-five years of Peace'. As my friend Xavier Muñoz wrote later, 'The war had finished, but peace had not arrived.' But just to break the conspiracy of silence could cost you your liberty or your job. Aureli Escarré, Abbot of Montserrat, the mountain-top monastery near Barcelona that is Catalonia's spiritual home, used his elevated position in the church to express the view that the years from 1939 to 1964 had been 25 years of victory rather than of peace. He was banished into exile.

Who were the dead that Raimon was singing about? Maybe those who accepted the regime without a murmur of protest, but maybe also those who had died either during the civil war or in the terrible vengeance that Franco brought down upon his political opponents in the aftermath of the war. Ambiguity and indirect, oblique reference, these were the tools of opposition, whether in poetry, prose or song. Joan Fuster's *Dictionary for the Idle* (1964) is a perfect example. The word 'silence' is in the dictionary, and Fuster comments: 'Often, in fact almost always, to remain silent is *also* to lie.' It is hard to believe that Raimon was unaware of what his fellow-Valencian had written just three years earlier. In the same book, Fuster writes of '... the unbending resistance the literary person should put up against the devious or menacing requirements of society'. This sounds like explicit criticism of the Franco regime, but occurs in a discussion of the work of Erasmus. Fuster leaves the intelligent reader to make a further connection, between the Dutch humanist Erasmus and the Valencian humanist Luis Vives, who, as we have seen, found it more convenient to live his adult life outside of Spain.

But for most people silence, forgetting, was a condition of everyday life imposed by the repressive Franco regime. The Catalan poet Salvador Espriu expressed this sense of internal exile in his 'Cançó de Capvespre' (Evening Song):

Però ara és nit.
i he quedat solitari
a la casa dels morts
que només jo recordo.

(But now it is night / and I've been left alone / in the house of the dead / whom only I remember)

The singer Raimon set this poem to music in the 1970s. As Manuel Vázquez Montalbán puts it in his book *Barcelonas*, 'In this context Espriu's verses came to express, whether the poet intended it or not, the melancholy which accompanied the prohibition of memory', although for Espriu it has a deeper spiritual sense of isolation and despair. Taking a longer view, it is as if history has contradicted Espriu: memory has endured and is not satisfied. The past will not go away.

For some years after the end of the Spanish Civil War, it was conventional for written accounts to spend many pages explaining the background to the war, to give an account of the conflict, and to end the story with the victory of Franco's rebels in 1939. A variation on this approach preferred to see the Spanish war morphing into the wider European conflict of 1939–45, an approach I have favoured in my previous writing on the subject. However, over the past decade, I have become persuaded of the case that a vital part of writing about the war is to include both the terrors of the regime itself and the processes of remembering and forgetting, especially in the years since Franco's death. Helen Graham's recent and very readable book *The Spanish Civil War: a very short introduction* is a good example. Graham makes the important point that there are direct and personal links between those who sought refuge in France at the end of the Spanish war and the European war against fascism: 'The *Maquis*, in its incipient stages in 1941 in the south-west of France, grew out of the practical military knowledge, skills and experience of Spanish Republican veterans.' In addition to the major contribution of Spanish republicans to the French Resistance, some veterans of the Spanish war found themselves fighting with the Free French forces in North Africa, including the famous march from Morocco to Chad across the Sahara Desert to enlist in General Leclerc's army which later fought alongside British troops in Libya and was then given pride of place when French forces entered Paris in 1944.

Graham also gives a good account of the historical memory debate in a section entitled 'Old memories, new histories', in other words the rewriting of history based on memory and experience, which she sees as central to building a democratic culture in Spain. Official memory in Spain for a long time recognised only those who were killed on the Franco side of the argument, as at the Valle de los Caídos (Valley of the Fallen) monument outside Madrid. Xavier Cercas, a Catalan novelist who writes in Castilian has the story of the trek across the Sahara at the heart of his novel (and later film) *Soldados de Salamina (Soldiers of Salamis)*. Miralles, the anti-hero of the novel, finds himself fighting for freedom and democracy (and a country that is not his own) in the middle of the desert with an ethnically mixed bunch of Free French soldiers. It is Miralles who is the 'soldier who saves civilisation' not (as he wished to be seen) General Franco. The extraordinary success of this novel at the turn of the twenty-first century indicated both that Spaniards had not forgotten the war, and that new interpretations were urgently needed, acknowledging atrocities committed on both sides of the divide.

Cercas has repudiated very publicly the *'pacto del olvido'* (pact of forgetting) that both right and left accepted in the years of the transition to democracy. Spain would be democratic, would look forward rather than back (*'el pasado bien pasado'* — leave the past in the past, as the old Castilian saying goes). Jorge Semprún, later Minister of Culture in the Madrid government, had prefigured this in the screenplay for Alain Resnais' film 'La Guerre est finie' (The War is Over, 1966). Semprún had left Spain with his family as a teenager in 1939, joined the Resistance in 1942 and was captured and held in the concentration camp at Buchenwald until 1945. His subsequent career as an underground Communist Party agitator in Spain (using the pseudonym Federico Sánchez, and under instruction from the party leadership in exile), is recounted in his bitter book *Communism in Spain in the Franco era: the autobiography of Federico Sánchez*. It is clear that the film, which argues that the leadership in exile has lost touch completely with social and economic developments in Spain, was directly based on Semprún's quarrel with Santiago Carrillo, the long-serving general-secretary of the party, whom he came to view as an egotistical falsifier of history.

Semprún's view, supported by the actual events of the 1970s transition from dictatorship to democracy, was that Spain was developing towards a liberal, capitalist democracy rather than a communist revolution. Yet in the long run, both men were linked in their desire to turn over a new leaf in Spanish history. Carrillo, by now a new-style Eurocommunist, was so keen to secure the democratic transition that he was a key figure on the Left of Spanish politics arguing for the 1978 Constitution with its clause about the irrevocable unity of Spain, a clause forced on the democratic politicians by the army in return for which they consented to be bound by the constitution.

This in turn is of course the source of the current quarrel between Catalonia and Spain, and the possibility of military intervention by the army in defence of the constitution has been raised as both a nightmare by the Left and threat by the Right.

Of course, any film by Alain Resnais is more complex than a mere recital of facts and events can suggest. In some ways the film is about the fragility, even the impossibility of memory. How can we enter the heads of those who were killed or tortured, or the friends and family members they left behind, the exiles who died in German concentration camps or built new lives for themselves in Latin America? In one of Michael Portillo's first excursions outside politics into the world of television documentary and travelogues, in 1998, he met up with some of the Spanish family from which his own branch had been separated by the war and exile. His father had been Professor of Civil Law at the University of Salamanca and had left Spain with the defeated Republican army in 1939, although one of his brothers was killed fighting on the rebel side. When Portillo suggested to camera that it was all a long time ago, and that ties of family were more important than those of political allegiance, there was an uneasy silence from the gathered members of the family. It was obvious, I would hope, to most viewers that they did not share this optimistic view that the 'war is over' and it was all a long time ago. Portillo himself has since written in a much more nuanced way about historical memory, as we shall see below.

In the little seaside village of Arenys de Mar, Salvador Espriu had never forgotten the war. In order to write about life in Franco's Spain, he developed a complicated, indirect pattern of associations which not only allowed him to comment on the present but to develop links with the past. One of his best-known books of poetry was *La Pell de Brau* (Bull Skin), where the title refers directly to Spain, since it is a common image for the shape of the Iberian Peninsula on a map. Spain is also Sepharad, the land from which the Sephardic Jews were exiled, while Sinera (Arenys with the letters reversed) is his home town of Arenys. Espriu writes of the people of Sepharad as if they too were in some kind of political exile, a kind of internal exile imposed by the Franco regime, and of course that sense of being a discounted part of Spain belongs especially to Catalan-speakers, whose language and traditions were being trampled on daily. He writes of this homeland (Spain? Catalonia? Greater Catalonia?):

Car sóc molt covard i salvatge
i estimo a més amb un
desesperat dolor
aquesta meva pobra,
bruta, trista, dissortada pàtria

(For I am cowardly and wild / and moreover I love / with a painful desperation / this poor country of mine, / dirty, gloomy and unlucky)

It is not an image that tourists to the Costa Brava in the 1950s and 1960s would have recognised, for it is a landscape of the mind and of the imagination.

Espriu, as Josep-Maria Castellet pointed out in a fine edition of his poems published in 1977, was much influenced in the sadness and pessimism of his work by the biblical Old Testament and the Jewish books of wisdom, especially *Job* and *Ecclesiastes*. The suffering and exiles of the Jewish people became symbolic of the sufferings of Sepharad/Spain. The writings of the Gerona Cabbala were becoming known as early as the 1920s, and from them Espriu derives some of his most important dualities: Darkness and Light; a Cruel God and a Loving God; Justice and Grace; Exile and Redemption. The notion of sacrifice, of the Suffering Servant, is there in the poem that begins:

De vegades és necesari i forçós
que un home mori por un poble,
però mai no ha de morir un poble
per un home sol.

(Sometimes it is absolutely necessary / for a man to die for a people, / but a people should never die / for the sake of just one man.)

Yet this poem is addressed to the whole of Spain, not just to the Catalans. In that sense, there is always the glow of a possible dawn in the darkest moment of pessimism:

Fes que siguin segurs els ponts del diàleg
i mira de comprendre i estimar
les raons i les parles diverses dels teus fills
…

Que Sepharad visqui eternament
en l'ordre i en la pau, en el treball,
en la difícil i merescuda
llibertat

(Keep open and strong the bridges of dialogue / and seek to understand and love / your children's reasons and languages / …

That Sepharad may live forever / in order and in peace, at work, / in hard-won and deserved / freedom.)

To argue openly in this way directly for difference, and for community and solidarity across difference, would have been anathema in Franco's Spain. For some Spaniards today, it is still so. As Daniel Conversi observed in his 1997 book *The Basques, the Catalans and Spain*: 'As the name "Sepharad" suggests, Spain could be emulated and desired only in its pre-1492 form (and) might one day recognise that pre-1492 form to be one of cultural dialogue and exchange, but now recast in the image of democracy and equality.' Indeed, and yet how saddened Espriu would be to find the bridges of dialogue in such poor condition, and misunderstanding and hatred once again between the peoples of Spain. Espriu kept that ideal alive, in a mythical little fishing village called Sinera, but his voice is a very quiet voice once more.

In another little fishing village on the Catalan coast, Norman Lewis in *Voices of the Old Sea*, noted in the post-Civil War period exactly why people in a small-sized community might want to forget. He tried to find out about a man who disappeared at the end of the war in 1939. Here 'silence and forgetfulness' are seen as ways of coping with external threats to the village: 'Whatever had happened here that might be seen as damaging to the community was in the process of being forgotten, and the memory of it would eventually be as wholly and utterly consumed as a corpse committed to the worms'.

The issue of the potentially divisive effect of memory on small communities is especially pertinent on Ibiza, which suffered very badly during the Civil War. The Ibizans themselves have been rather reticent about the war and its impact, but a number of the foreign writers who have passed through the island have noted both the facts of the matter and the impact on the people who survived. Laurie Lee noted in a 1959 *Encounter* article: 'The War festered here as violently as anywhere — perhaps more so in its isolation — and though twenty-odd years had passed since that time, the village still smarted with it, and people still told you about it, though with lowered voices ...' He meets a woman who was on the 'winning' side; her brother and son, both Civil Guards, had been shot by the republicans, but she had not forgotten the hunger and starvation amongst the defeated: 'There was murder, yes; prisoners were shot; there (were) many thrown over the cliffs. A few escaped with crippled limbs — you'll still see them about today.'

Ibiza had a bad war. Initially its elite (church, land-owners, Civil Guards) had declared for the rebels. Then the republicans had got organised and rounded up the known fascists on the island, imprisoning them in the castle at Ibiza Town. The North American journalist and author Elliot Paul observed events at first hand in the village of Santa Eulàlia del Riu and wrote about them in *The Life and Death of a Spanish Town* (1937). The republicans had initially used Ibiza as a base from which to secure the loyalty of Mallorca. The involvement of the Italian air-force and developments on the mainland had made this difficult and the republicans retreated to Ibiza. Paul writes of a Sunday morning bombing raid (13 September 1936) that killed mainly women and children along the promenade of Ibiza Town. It is at this point that he reports one of the fascist prisoners telling his anarchist guards "Our turn is coming now." Whatever the flash-point may have been, up to one hundred of the prisoners in the castle were killed, the remainder escaping through the windows.

By this time, the main priority for the republican government was the defence of Madrid, now under siege by rebel forces camped in its university city on the northwestern outskirts. The order was given to evacuate the remaining loyal troops and militiamen from Ibiza. The rebels took control and there was a general round-up of anyone and everyone remaining on the island who was known to have left-wing views. It was blood-letting on a large scale for such a tiny island. A Norwegian writer, Leif Borthen, returned to the subject of Civil War Ibiza in his 1967 book *The Road to San Vicente*, now available in English translation. Borthen writes: 'When I tentatively broached the subject of what had happened in San Vicente during the Civil War no one was willing to speak. These people are by nature as tight-lipped as any Norwegian mountain peasant and would never talk about intimate affairs or give away family secrets.' (By contrast, Paul's 'indiscretion and naming of names' had caused many problems on the island subsequent to its publication.) It emerged that the victims in Sant Vicent had been 10–12 people shot by the rebels, while the Republicans had killed the parish priest and 'the Frenchman'. Gradually — and this is the real subject of Borthen's book — it emerges that the Frenchman was none other than Raoul Villain, who in July 1914 had assassinated the great French socialist leader and founder of the newspaper

L'Humanité, Jean Jaurès. His relatives had managed to get him released from a mental hospital and had banished him to Ibiza. Within the village he had been known as a harmless eccentric.

If events on Ibiza were dramatic and violent, the other two Balearic Islands fared very differently. On Mallorca, an expeditionary force sent from Ibiza to secure the island for the republic was rapidly repulsed, and Mallorca became a major base for the Italian air-force from which they would later launch murderous bombing raids against Barcelona and Valencia. As for Menorca, that backwater of history, it remained in republican hands throughout the war and largely peaceful. All this came to an abrupt end in 1939. Some republicans fled to France, especially those who had been actively working for the collectivisation of agriculture and industry, but many remained in Menorca. Most holiday-makers on Menorca do the boat trip round Mahon harbour. But the tour guides never speak about the imprisonment of large numbers of republicans in brutal conditions in the forts around the harbour at the end of the Civil War.

Elsewhere in Greater Catalonia, the end of the war gave way to many revenge killings. The main route of the rebels' advance in 1938/39 was into Catalonia, while most of Valencia remained in republican hands. The intention had been to evacuate republicans by sea, but the republican navy set sail for Bizerta in North Africa before many of those who feared for their lives in Franco's Spain could reach the ports. Many thousands of refugees were stranded in ports such as Alicante and Valencia, some escaping by boat, but others herded into concentration camps. José Peirats, author of the best account of the war from a libertarian perspective (*Anarchists in the Spanish revolution*) contrasted the 'generous and simple peace of soldiers' as troops fraternised at Madrid at the end of the war with the disastrous failure to evacuate republicans from Alicante and the subsequent settling of scores by the rebels.

The events on Ibiza and Menorca could no doubt be replicated in many other small communities in Spain. In the areas that remained loyal to the republic, many of the reprisals happened after the end of the war. Paul Preston, Franco's biographer, estimates 200,000 prisoners executed between 1939 and 1943. The dubious legal basis of this was the Law of Responsibilities passed in early 1939. 'Crimes' included crimes of commission (membership of left-wing parties and Masonic lodges) but crimes of omission too ('those ... who have opposed the National Movement by either deed or grave passivity'). Much use was made of summary military tribunals, and 110,000 of these were held in Catalonia in the years immediately following the war.

Part of the forgetting was exactly what the war had been about. It has often been suggested that Hugh Thomas's history of the Civil War was the book that Spaniards were unable to write, with its view of the events of 1936–1939 as 'the culmination of one hundred years of class war'. Equally, Ken Loach's 1995 film 'Land and Freedom' was the film that the Spanish were unable to make. It confronts the key issues of what was at stake socially and economically in the war, and the methods used to achieve those ends. In placing the theme of social revolution in the foreground, Loach follows Orwell quite closely, though the detailed village discussions about collectivisation and the feminist positions put forward by the militiawoman Blanca go far beyond anything in *Homage to Catalonia*. Dave Carr in Loach's film is a member of the Communist Party, so what he comes to recognise is not just the primacy of revolution but the extent to which the Communist Party is an obstacle to it. Orwell had become convinced of this too, especially through the events of May 1937 in Barcelona, when the communists turned on the anarchists and libertarian socialists of POUM (Orwell was in a POUM militia). Carr writes to his girlfriend at home in Liverpool: 'The Party stinks ... it is evil and corrupt ... Stalin is just using the

126

working class like pieces on a chess-board to be bartered, used and sacrificed.' Certainly by 1937, social revolution was taking second place to simply 'winning the war'. In the event, the republicans achieved neither objective.

What else, then, might we remember? One little noted feature of the 1930s in Spanish history is the start of the process of relative emancipation of women. At the beginning of the republican period, the Catholic Church supported votes for women on the basis that it considered them to be more likely to vote for parties which had strong Catholic and conservative leanings. Ironically the republicans blocked votes for women on the same basis, and it was not until 1933 that they were given the vote. In one powerful passage from *The Life and Death of a Spanish Town*, Elliott Paul contrasts the hope that had existed with the betrayal and loss of hope in the reality of war: 'It was in their eager faces that could be seen a new and better Spain. Their poise and curiosity, their dignity, the cut of their clothes placed a hedge between their era and the shawls, kerchiefs and thick petticoats of their mothers.' Throughout Greater Catalonia, women educated themselves and their children to want more, to expect more from life than the limited world they had inherited. On the Aragon Front, women like Blanca in 'Land and Freedom' fought alongside men. I remember distant conversations on a Barcelona market with a woman from Castellon who had grown to womanhood in the 1930s and regretted what she saw as the closing in again of possibilities for the young, and especially for girls. On Mallorca, Lucia Graves also noted the way life had shuttered around girls of her generation, and the new possibilities aroused by the contact with young women from other parts of Europe.

The 1930s raised people's expectations of what might be expected from government. Henry Buckley was a Catholic, inclined to conservatism, the correspondent in Spain for the *Daily Telegraph*. But he loved the church of social concern rather than the institutionalised Spanish church of the ABC (army, bishops, crown). For Buckley, democracy meant more education, health care, land reform, just the policies the Catalan Generalitat, the autonomous Catalan government set up under the second Spanish Republic of 1931–1939, was working on at the outbreak of war. His book *The Life and Death of the Spanish Republic* has had a difficult history. Published in 1940, almost the entire stock was lost when a London warehouse was bombed in 1940. Republished in 2013 with an introduction by Paul Preston, it does credit to a humane and talented journalist.

If many of the personal experiences of the war were too difficult to remember, there were other memories which entered into the collective store and were never erased, as Henry Buckley correctly predicted in 1940. All the major Mediterranean ports were bombed, especially by Italians based in Mallorca but also by Germans: Barcelona, Castellon, Valencia, Gandia and Alicante. For a war reporter, ports could be seen as legitimate targets, but he deplored the bombing of civilians. 'That hatred', he wrote, 'will last many years, it may have strange results in years to come.' Certainly neither Guernica nor Barcelona has forgotten. On 26 April 1937, the German air-force had destroyed Guernica. The town had no air defences, and was crowded with refugees and retreating soldiers from the rebels' assault on Bilbao. Hugh Thomas suggests that only 10% of the town was left undamaged and puts the death-toll at 1,000 in a town whose normal population was 7,000. Such are the stark facts behind Picasso's 'Guernica', one of the angriest and most emblematic paintings of the twentieth century.

On 28 January 1938, the Italian air-force launched a massive raid on Barcelona from their base in Mallorca. The city was poorly prepared. The Italians attacked again on 30 January. The bombers came again on 16 March, and the German ambassador to Spain reported to Berlin that 'All parts of the city were affected. There was no evidence of any attempt to hit military objectives' (in

Thomas, *The Spanish Civil War*). On the morning of 17 March, Júlia Gay was killed by a bomb while out shopping. She was the mother of the novelists Juan and Luis Goytisolo, and the poet José Augustín Goytisolo. Luis was still a baby. These bombing raids were undertaken without consultation, mainly by the Italians but with support from the Germans and Ramón Franco's rebel air force. Franco himself asked for them to be stopped, concerned about the possible effect on non-intervention if the killing were continued and became widely known abroad. In these raids against civilian targets, 1,300 were killed and over two thousand injured. For Josep Trueta, chief surgeon at Barcelona's main hospital, the raids were like Guernica, 'meant to test the population's capacity of resistance. By the time they ended, there were 2,200 casualties in my hospital.'

Portbou is in many ways one of the byways of the cruel and violent history of the twentieth century, a small railway station quarried out of the cliffs where North and South Catalonia (some might prefer to say France and Spain) meet. The trains still hurry to and fro, but it does not give the impression of being a place where anything ever happens. The retreating Republican army used in the main the road crossing into France and exile at Le Perthus, where the motorway now crosses the border too. Others crossed with the army, including the great Spanish poet Antonio Machado, who had rather reluctantly thrown in his lot with the elected government (his brother made the opposite decision and supported Franco and the rebels). He survived only a few days and is buried in the cemetery at Collioure, within sight of the railway line. The links are everywhere: Salvador Allende, then a young minister in the Chilean government, later to die in a hail of bullets in a USA-inspired coup, arranged for 2,500 of the republicans caught in the French concentration camps to be shipped to Chile. The small kindnesses, the humanitarian urge, were part of that short and brutish century.

In Portbou itself, the German philosopher Walter Benjamin is remembered, though it has taken some time. They were not good times to be a Jew. Exiled in France, he wrote from Paris in 1935: 'Actually, I hardly feel constrained to try to make head or tail of this condition of the world. On this planet a great number of civilisations have perished in blood and horror.' Things got worse. The Germans invaded France and Benjamin found his flat and his library impounded by the Gestapo. He fled south, hoping to escape to America via Lisbon. He already had an 'emergency visa' to enter the USA and a transit visa for Spain. But no exit visa for France. Benjamin arrived in Portbou across the mountains. The nine-hour hike striking inland from the seaside town of Banyuls, up over the mountains, and down into Portbou must have been a nightmare for Benjamin, a sick man, and notoriously clumsy. The assumption is that Benjamin, convinced that the following day he would be returned to occupied France, took his life that night in a hotel in Portbou. That, at any rate, is the story. Life was cheap in 1940 and suicide was as convenient an explanation as any.

As Benjamin's reputation has grown in a new century set on repeating the disasters of the old century, some people still wonder about the truth. Benjamin had experimented with consciousness-altering drugs on the island of Ibiza in 1932. He regularly took morphine in relation to a heart condition. At least three possibilities remain: suicide (which may have been despair at the state of Europe, or personal despair at the prospect of being sent back to France); an accidental overdose; a political murder by Nazi agents collaborating with Franco's police. Local people clubbed together to provide a monument to Benjamin in 1979, though this is now overshadowed by a monument designed by the Israeli artist Dani Karavan, and paid for (if rather reluctantly) by the German government. It is a kind of anti-memorial, reminding us in German, English, Spanish and Catalan of another of Benjamin's thoughts: 'It is more arduous to honour the memory of the nameless than that of the renowned. Historical construction is devoted to the memory of the nameless.' Karavan has sought to remember at Portbou all those who died and continue to die because of their race, their religion, their ideas, and the mere accident of being the wrong person in the wrong place at the wrong moment.

Benjamin was not the only person who passed through Portbou en route to his death. During that October of 1940, a number of prominent Republican exiles in France were handed over to the Spanish authorities by the Gestapo. Franco did not mess with political prisoners. The most prominent victim, and the one whose death inscribed the most bloody wound across the second half of the Catalan twentieth century was Lluís Companys. Companys had served an apprenticeship on the left as a lawyer in the 1920s with CNT, the anarcho-syndicalist trade union which dominated working-class politics in the towns and villages of Catalonia, and as a founder member of the trade union (*Unió de Rabassaires*) which represented the Catalan peasants and argued for the urgency of land reform. His party was Esquerra Republicana Catalana, the Catalan Republican Left, a party that dominated Catalan politics in the 1930s, and now plays a vital in the Catalan independence debate. In January 1934 Companys succeeded to the Presidency of the Generalitat. He remained its President throughout the years of the military rebellion and then in exile.

The seizure of Companys by the Gestapo after the German invasion of France, his hurried return to Barcelona, the secret trial at Montjuïc Castle on 14 October, and the summary execution and burial in a common paupers' grave on 15 October were supposed to set an end to an epoch. But Catalonia had acquired a martyr, and martyrs are an integral part of public memory. The writer Juan Goytisolo knew the story, and in *Señas de Identidad* (*Marks of Identity*), first published in Mexico in 1966, Goytisolo ends with a confrontation on

131

Montjuïc. The violence is all inward, a writer preparing for exile while the official guides peddle lies about the recent history of his country. He slips a one hundred peseta note to a gardener who silently leads him to the spot where President Companys was shot in October 1940.

It takes an effort to find the common grave where Companys is buried, above the glass niches and mausoleums of other honest citizens in the sprawling public cemetery at Montjuïc. El Fossar de la Pedrera is a steep-sided old quarry with high, bare, creamy-coloured walls. The entrance is up a flight of steps through a grove of cypress-trees and simple square stone posts, inscribed with the names of the many who were shot and buried here in the blood-letting that ended the Spanish war: four thousand judicial murders to celebrate Franco's victory. It is a journey from darkness to light, from forgetfulness to remembrance in the implacable clarity of the Mediterranean sun. Memorials have blossomed at El Fossar de la Pedrera, as part of the process of remembering: the Austrian Civil War volunteers, the guerrillas who carried on the struggle after 1940, a man whose mother was buried here in the common grave because no-one had the money or cared enough to give her proper burial. The Companys memorial itself is a bridge over water, as if emphasising the continuity from the democratic republic of the 1930s to the autonomous Catalonia of today, and the uncertainty of tomorrow.

For some years after the re-establishment of democracy in Spain, it was all about forgetting — the *pacto del olvido*. But since the 1990s there has been a determined movement within civil society to remember, not just in a private, grief-stricken way, but in a public way. Finally, people want to know what happened to neighbours, friends, family members killed either in the war or in the harsh repression of the Franco years. Many of the victims were buried in unmarked common graves, and the opening up of such graves and attempts to identify the bodies have been features of the movement, co-ordinated by the awkwardly named *Asociación para la Recuperación de la Memoria Histórica* (Society for the Recovery of Historical Memory). The movement received political support from the socialist Prime Minister, José Luis Rodríguez Zapatero, whose father was an army captain shot in 1936 for refusing to join the military rebellion. In his will he described his creed as 'love for peace, for good and for improving the living conditions of the lower classes'. The 2007 Law of Historical Memory has paved the way to official opening of common war-graves (there are 179 in Catalonia alone), for appeals against arbitrary military tribunal verdicts and the removal at long last of remaining Franquist symbols from public buildings. It cannot bring back the dead but it has been a healing process for many Spaniards. Passed by a socialist government, the law is the other side of the coin from the public memory of the Franco years which commemorated only those who had died or suffered in the rebel cause. Yet Javier Cercas reminded us in *Soldiers of Salamis* that the supporters of the Republic also committed atrocities, as on Ibiza. Indeed, the action of the novel is driven by the central character's failure to shoot an escaping fascist prisoner in the last days of the war. It is as hard within politically divided communities to find common ground on memory as on any other issue.

A further Act of Parliament in 2007, known as the 'Grandchildren's Law', has extended Spanish citizenship to a quarter of a million descendants of Spaniards who left Spain and lost their nationality at the end of the Civil War. Most of the applications have been by grown-up children and grandchildren living in Latin American countries. The purpose of this law was to 'recognize and extend rights and to establish measures in favour of those who have been victims of political persecution or violence during the Civil War and the Dictatorship'. While these were measures passed by a socialist government, the subsequent conservative government has also been active

133

in the historical memory stakes. It was they who passed the 2014 law giving automatic Spanish citizenship to Jewish people who can prove they are the descendants of Jews expelled from Spain in 1492 and before, whether or not they wish to live in Spain. Numbers involved are relatively small but predictably this measure has raised energetic reactions in Muslim circles, with some commentators demanding equal treatment for the rather larger number of descendants of the Moriscos, expelled between 1609 and 1614. It has been calculated that there as many as five million descendants of Moriscos in Morocco alone.

Giles Tremlett has dealt with the issue of historical memory in some detail in his book *Ghosts of Spain* (2006), dedicating his first chapter to the *secretos a voces* (whispered secrets) which even before the passing of the 2007 law were beginning to come out into the open. He saw it as the search for truth, rather than revenge. In 2009, Michael Portillo made a documentary for BBC Television called 'Digging up the Dead'. In this he argued for fairness in the treatment of victims on both sides of the conflict, even going so far as to admit that whereas many of the killings on the republican side had been moments of mob violence, 'on Franco's side, murder was official policy. He boasted that he wanted to conquer Spain "centimetre by centimetre" to eliminate all those who did not support his coup'. This was published in an on-line version of the *Daily Mail* and they are strong words for a right-wing politician. Yet he refused to recognise that exhumations of bodies was a sensible way forward, preferring to propose a general recognition of historical wrongs: 'Spain needs politicians and public on either side to accept that blame for past atrocities is widely spread. Horrendous acts of barbarism were committed. The time to investigate and to punish has gone. But the time quietly to respect the dead has come.' Perhaps it is better to leave these matters to the Spanish themselves. In 2003, Portillo's Scottish mother, Cora de Portillo, unveiled a blue plaque at Westfield House in Oxfordshire commemorating the 30 Basque children exiled from their homeland who had been cared for there during the war. She had worked there as a volunteer. It is a quieter but no less effective way of commemorating the past.

Within Spain too, remembering has included the rehabilitation of figures never mentioned under the Franco regime. One such is Josep Renau. Renau was a Valencian communist artist who used photomontage in poster and collage work, doubtless inspired in part by the *avant garde* of Soviet artists in Russia in the 1920s. He became director of fine art in the republic, and was the man who commissioned 'Guernica' for the 1937 exhibition in Paris from Picasso. He was also responsible for the photomontages displayed at the same exhibition and many posters in support of the Republic. He organised the evacuation of the treasures of Madrid's Prado Museum, where they were at risk of bombing. They were brought to the Torres de Serrano in Valencia and when Valencia too became a bombing target, they were moved on to Switzerland via Figueres. Renau fared worse than the Prado paintings: he was interned in the bleak camp at Argelès in North Catalonia, from where he obtained a visa to go to Mexico. From 1958 he was based in East Berlin where he died in 1982.

The Civil War involved many people from outside of Spain, but its aftermath was a uniquely Spanish tragedy. For the two generations of Spaniards who had lived their lives under Franco, there were still so many unanswered questions. Even before the end of the Franco regime, films were suggesting some of the violence and repression at the heart of Spanish society. Víctor Erice's 1973 film 'El Espíritu de la Colmena' (The Spirit of the Beehive) is a complex and heart-rending film full of symbolism about a very young girl befriending a wounded republican soldier who is later captured and shot. Since 1976, books and films about the Spanish War, often preserving the innocent child's-eye point of view, have been an important way in which people, individually and as a society, have begun to come to terms with what happened.

Commercially they are very successful. On the one hand they tug at people's emotions, tell strong stories and look good on the screen. For similar reasons, they travel well, too. But on the other hand, there is little doubt that people of all ages need to understand how and why Franco came to power, and why the best efforts of opposition within and outside Spain failed to shift him.

Notable among such films which have been successful both in Spain and abroad is Guillermo del Toro's 'Pan's Labyrinth', in which the fantasies of a young girl both contrast with and parallel the heartless violence of the adult world. Its context was the ongoing guerrilla warfare waged in remote mountainous areas in the 1940s and repressed with much brutality. José Luis Cuerda's 'La lengua de las mariposas' (Butterfly Tongue) is based on a number of short novels by the Galician writer Manuel Rivas. It concerns the relationship of a young boy and his progressive teacher in a small Galician village. At the end of the film the teacher is rounded up with other leftist suspects and taken away to be shot.

Within Catalonia, a series of films in both Catalan and Spanish have contributed to the post-1975 recovery of historical memory, as Jaume Martí-Olivella makes clear in an excellent essay in Dominic Keown's 2011 edited volume *A Companion to Catalan Culture*. These include 'The Burnt City' (La ciutat cremada, Antoni Ribas, 1976) about the events of Barcelona's Tragic Week in 1909, 'The Old Memory' (La vieja memoria, Jaime Camino) concerning memories of Civil War survivors, and 'Companys, Catalonia on Trial' (Companys, procés a Catalunya, Josep Maria Forn, 1979) about the show trial of the President of the Generalitat in 1940. These films were made on small budgets for small audiences in the first years of the transition to democracy. Manuel Huerga's 'Salvador' is more recent, made in 2006 and concerns the last Catalan victim of Franco, Salvador Puig Antich, a young anarchist garrotted in 1974. Huerga says of this film: 'It is a film that can help to exorcize many things and to confront many ghosts by forcing us to see face to face some things that had been hidden from us or that people were afraid to confront.'

Perhaps it is too early for the great film that I sense is still there to be made, the 'War and Peace' of the Spanish twentieth century that seems not quite over yet. Memory is laid down in layers of sediment and has not yet acquired a sufficiently solid form that most Spaniards (here I include Catalans, Valencians and islanders) might recognise as including the experience of their own families. Necessarily, memory looks back, and yet quite rightly most people in Greater Catalonia seem much more concerned with their present and future than with their past. Yet to quote Manuel Huerga again: 'These things are a part of our past and we must know our past in order to see where we are going.'

Chapter 6
Mind your Language

(Joan) Maragall for example was at once cause and effect of his Catalonia. Let us not forget that in his conception, the country is "mother' and "daughter" of its people: it is what we receive and what moulds us, and that which we mould as we make it: at once a legacy and an undertaking.

(Joan Fuster, 'Maragall and Unamuno, face to face', in J.M. Sobrer, Catalonia: a self-portrait, 1992. Translation by Sobrer)

1. The development and use of Catalan

Phoenicians, Greeks, Carthaginians had all traded with the country we now call Spain. The Roman Empire was a rather different matter. The Romans occupied the land, gave it a culture, a language, a territorial organisation and roads. Latin became not just the language of the conquerors but of the conquered. The only exception was that of the Basques, but that is another story. This Latin had little to do with the Latin that until recently was taught in our schools, or recited in Catholic churches throughout Europe, the language which in the Middle Ages was the language of scholarship and diplomacy as well as the Christian religion. Classical Latin is a sophisticated written language, but what we are dealing with in post-Roman Spain is a fairly large number of local dialects of spoken, or Vulgar, Latin. Vulgar because it is the language of the common people. But the Vulgar Latin (perhaps we should say Latins) of the native Iberians was strong enough to absorb the languages of settlers such as the Visigoths, and to become a common everyday language of Al-Andalus after 700, spoken both by the Mozarabs who continued to practice Christianity and by those who converted to Islam for whatever reason. What little we know about Mozarabic comes from transcriptions in Arabic script, since the educated classes spoke and wrote in Arabic. It was some version of Mozarabic that we assume was spoken in the lands of Greater Catalonia south of the Ebro which were under Muslim rule for long centuries. However, it is probable that over the centuries, Arabic came to largely replace Mozarabic as the everyday language of all three communities of Al-Andalus — Christian, Jewish and Muslim. On Mallorca, the Mozarabic language survived long enough to give such local oddities as the place-name ending –utz (pronounced /ooch/ as in Fornalutx — the place of the forge).

The various Vulgar Latins were known as Romance, and in the north-east corner of Iberia, a new Romance language emerged which by the dawn of the Middle Ages had become known as Catalan. It had considerable similarities with Occitan and other Southern French languages/dialects, and the early Catalan poets used Provençal, the language of the troubadours, in preference to Catalan as a literary language. Catalan acquired cohesion and dynamism as the Counts of Barcelona gradually came to dominate the geographical space north and south of the Eastern Pyrenees, eventually becoming a language of literature and commerce as well as the daily language of people. This process is important as by definition a 'Vulgar' language is a spoken language, the language of the street and the market-place, and the achievement of Catalan was to become a respectable written language as well, although scholars such as Ramon Llull also used Arabic and Latin.

The spread and development of the Catalan language is closely allied to political and historical developments outlined in chapter 1. As we saw there, the Crown of

Aragon with its twin capitals in Saragossa and Barcelona, included both Aragonese and Catalans. The Aragonese spoke a dialect of Castilian Spanish which is now confined to the mountains of Huesca province, while the Catalans spoke, well, Catalan. Thus as the conquest of Muslim lands went forward, Aragonese soldiers, and later settlers, were more likely to be found in the inland areas while Catalan soldiers and settlers tended to dominate the process along the coast. For this reason, some of the inland areas of the Valencian Community have always been Castilian-speaking. Down towards Murcia some Castilian towns such as Villena or Orihuela ended up incorporated into the Kingdom of Valencia. A further complication in terms of modern borders is the Aragonese *Franja* (borderlands) where Catalan is quite widely used in villages which are included in the modern-day autonomous region of Aragon.

Catalan did not develop evenly as a language. Once the crowns of Aragon and Castile had united, Catalan gradually fell out of fashion as a literary language, and when trade and commerce revived in the eighteenth century, the language used was Castilian. It was not until the nineteenth century that possible use of the language in its written form became a live subject. A Catalan grammar appeared in 1814, a New Testament in 1832 and in 1833 Carles Aribau's 'Oda a la Pàtria' (Patriotic Ode). This was a key event linking once and for all the question of national identity with the national language. But despite all the efforts of grammarians and linguists, it proved difficult to establish a standard spoken or written form of the language. Thus Valencian continued to have observable differences from Catalan in North and South Catalonia, a difference often referred to by linguists as the western and eastern tendencies. The correct pronunciation of Barcelona is similar in English and Catalan, because the Catalans pronounce the final unstressed 'a' as the 'neutral vowel' sound /ə/. Similarly unstressed 'o' becomes /u/. Valencians do not use these vowel changes. The Catalan possessives *meva/teva/seva* become *meua/teua/seua*, with the written 'u' pronounced /w/. There are also some differences in vocabulary. Although the Catalan of the Balearic Islands should accord to the eastern tendency in the language, notable differences have developed over time, especially in a feature as everyday as the definite article. So Catalan el/la/l' are replaced by *es/sa/s'* in the singular, while the plural forms *els/les* are replaced by *ets* or *es* for masculine nouns and *ses* in the feminine. These forms derive from Latin *ipse* (self) and the frequency of the 's' sound in daily conversation lends a particular note to spoken Mallorquí, Menorquí and Eivissenc.

There is general agreement now that Catalan is a single language, with dialects, although these dialects have their own names so that, for example, a Catalan-speaker on Menorca is more likely to say 'parlo menorquí' (I speak Menorcan) than 'parlo català'. Traditionally, Catalan has been regulated and standardised by the Institut d'Estudis Catalans in Barcelona, but there are now separate bodies carrying out this process in Valencia and the Balearic Islands, including recognising regional variants, and even for the town of L'Alguer (Alghero) on Sardinia. In that sense, and despite the regional variations, Catalan is closer to the French notion of a regulatory body determining what is 'proper French' than to the rather casual 'anything goes' approach of English.

The Balearic Islands and Valencia have played an important role in the process of making Catalan a fit language for the modern world: education, literature and science. In 1901 a Mallorcan priest, Antoni-Maria Alcover made a public announcement inviting contributions to a dictionary that eventually extended to ten volumes. He convened a Linguistic Congress in 1906, attended by 3,000 people. Alcover died in 1932, and the dictionary was completed decades later in 1963 by a Menorcan, Francesc de Borja Moll. Alcover was interested in what we might call the natural history of languages, and along the way to composing his dictionary collected many Mallorcan folk-tales. In the southern area of the Valencian Community, an important collaborator in the dictionary project was Enric Valor, a son of Castalla, imprisoned 1966-68 for political activities in support of the Valencian language. In the foyer of the Castalla secondary school that carries his name is a plaque announcing: 'Since I was very young, I have been very conscious of language: proud to speak and write in a dignified way this very solid Catalan of the Foia de Castalla.' The *Diccionari Català/Valencià/Balear* (DCVB) starts not from the premise that Catalan is one language with dialectical forms, but that what we mean by the Catalan language is the sum total of its usage in Greater Catalonia. It is disappointing to find this perspective so often ignored by people trying to use language issues to score political points. Like all the best dictionaries, the DCVB is always going to be an incomplete work with additions and corrections still being added. It is available on the internet and in printed form.

* * * * * * *

In the autonomous region of Catalonia, a key to the ongoing political success of nationalist parties has been the way in which language and national identity have become tightly entwined. This neatly avoids the exclusivism of a nationalism based on ethnic identity. Anyone can be a Catalan, simply by living there — and making a reasonable stab at learning the language. The 1983 Law of Linguistic Normalisation recognised that Catalan and Castilian are both official languages of Catalonia, and that citizens in their dealings with the state have the right to use which language they prefer. Yet the bulk of the law is concerned with establishing the circumstances under which Catalan might once again become the normal, everyday language of administration, commerce, education and civil society. For example, Article Two states that: 'Catalan is Catalonia's own language. All its citizens have the right to know the language and express themselves in it, both verbally and in writing, in their everyday lives and in public acts, both official and unofficial. This right implies, above all, being able to address Government bodies, public organisations, and public and private enterprises in Catalan either verbally or in writing; express oneself in Catalan at all meetings; carry out professional, labour, political, and trade union activities and receive schooling in Catalan.'

Such a major linguistic change does not take place overnight. After all, the Catalans have been trying to reverse a decline lasting centuries in a single generation. There are clear differences in people's ability to use Catalan effectively. Regular social surveys show that the ability to understand is the most generalised, while smaller percentages can speak the language, read it or write it. In Catalonia and the Balearic Islands, well over 90% of the population understand Catalan, while in Valencia and North Catalonia these figures decline to something over two-thirds. While nearly 90% in Catalonia are confident about speaking the language, these figures decline to three-quarters in the Balearic Islands, a little over a half in Valencia and under a half in North Catalonia. Similarly while most people in Catalonia and the Balearics can read Catalan, the figure in Valencia is about a half and in North Catalonia about one third.

When the 1983 language law was passed, only about one-third of Catalans were confident of their ability to write the language. The Generalitat has provided an extensive linguistic advice service for firms and for public agencies, advising them of correct translations and terminology. Catalan publishers have normally employed, in addition to the usual copy-editors and proof-readers, an additional linguistic specialist who would vet the text for correctness. Thus even while Catalan was being extolled as the normal language of use, its proponents were still honing it to be fit for purpose. The figure of those able to write Catalan has now climbed to two-thirds, in marked contrast to Valencian where there has been much less support for the language from the autonomous government, and just over one quarter are able to write the language.

The issue of schooling in Catalan has been a central one. Families from other parts of Spain who used Castilian in most of their home and work dealings were surprisingly enthusiastic about their children learning Catalan at school, and not just because speaking Catalan extended the range of their children's friendships. In contrast to Valencia and the islands, where Castilian had come to be seen as the 'desirable' language, the language of those who get on in society and at work, the existence in Catalonia of a large and powerful Catalan-speaking middle-class made Catalan seem the language of prestige. It is only in recent years that a concerted political campaign orchestrated by the Popular Party and the Spanish government has encouraged some Castilian-speaking families to demand that their children should have the right to be educated in Castilian.

The continuing success of the Catalan nationalists running the Generalitat in carrying through a radical and initially controversial language policy in schools has not been without its difficulties. An extensive programme of teacher-training was required in order to familiarise all teachers in Catalonia with the language, since not all had Catalan as their mother-tongue. In secondary, further and higher education, it has taken a considerable time for suitable text-books to appear or to be translated into Catalan. In higher education, teachers often use specialist text-books written in English. The language policy is the envy of many other minority languages in Europe. Children in Catalonia begin schooling in Catalan, with Castilian introduced as a second language in primary school (even though it may be the child's first language at home). This means that for young Catalans, there is no language problem, just a continual and usually unconscious mental juggling about when one language is appropriate and when the other. Indeed the general impression is that while there is a language issue for some older people, and certainly for some politicians, bilingualism is experienced as 'normal' for younger people, as indeed it is in most countries in the world.

The enormous increase in the use of Catalan as an administrative, educational and cultural language was one of the main challenges facing any visitor to Catalonia during the years after the establishment of the Catalan autonomous government, especially for those who had known Catalonia during the Franco years, when public life was dominated by Castilian, with Catalan reserved for private spaces such as the family. By 1990 there were newspapers and magazines in Catalan, a thriving Catalan publishing industry, radio and television in Catalan, *EastEnders* in Catalan (for some reason often held up as a sign that Catalan had arrived as a world language). By European standards, Catalan is a big language, though exactly how big no-one quite knows. One might begin by citing the six million inhabitants of South Catalonia, with deductions for those with limited fluency. Then one might add in those in the Catalan-speaking populations of the Balearic Islands, Valencia, Andorra, Alghero (Sardinia) and North Catalonia (Catalunya Nord). In round numbers, probably some 10 million out of a total 14 million population of Greater Catalonia can be taken as speakers of one version or other of Catalan.

The present position of Catalan has not been achieved without a struggle. Helena Drysdale, whose 2001 volume *Mother Tongues* remains a good source for understanding the situation of linguistic minorities in Europe, was optimistic based on field-work in the 1990s. She wrote that 'Castilian (speaking) immigrants have always learned Catalan with ease, and quickly become Catalans themselves, unlike the Castilian immigrants into the Basque

Country who find themselves faced with a language unlike any they have ever encountered. And unlike the Basques, who traditionally feared that their language, their race — and their morals — would be corrupted by incomers, the Catalans have embraced immigrant workers and turned them into fellow Catalans'. This leads on to a further crucial point. While Castilian Spanish and Basque are mutually exclusive languages (like English and Welsh), Castilian and Catalan have common roots and share many grammatical features and vocabulary.

This question of intelligibility between languages is controversial and demonstrates how political and social issues insert themselves continually and insistently into the neat categories of linguists. Why, for example, can I go to Italy and chatter happily in Spanish with a few Italians words thrown in, whereas in Portugal visitors who attempt to use Spanish are sternly told that Portuguese is a separate language? Happy memories return of bilingual nights out in Barcelona with people partying in the language (Castilian, Catalan) which came easier to them. Similarly, writers in the Catalan-speaking countries may choose to write in either of their languages, or use the languages for different purposes, for different kinds of writing. While for some writers such as Joan Fuster who had been struggling to publish in Catalan during the dictatorship, the return of democracy increased their resolve to continue writing in their first language, others such as Manuel Vázquez Montalbán who already had a readership for their Castilian books continued to write in Castilian. Barcelona in particular is a major publishing centre for books in Spanish as well as Catalan.

For some writers, choice of language is unproblematic. Javier Cercas, author of *Soldiers of Salamis*, told me "I write in Castilian because it's the language of my parents, it's the language we speak at home — well, of course I speak Catalan to my wife. But it's not been a difficulty for me, rather a spontaneous choice to write in Spanish." Conducting the interview in his university office, it was clear that his wife was not the only person he spoke to in Catalan, since we were interrupted during our interview by several of his students speaking Catalan and addressing him as Xavier, the Catalan form of his first name.

In some ways, cultural nationalists in Catalonia are less critical of writers who choose to write in Castilian than of writers whose work reflects the complicated bilingual nature of everyday life in Greater Catalonia. Kathryn Crameri has made an important contribution to our knowledge of Catalan literature with her book *Language, the Novelist and National Identity in Post-Franco Catalonia*, published in 2000. She emphasises how difficult and controversial the writer's choice of language is. Or rather, how intuitive, how easy such a choice might be if it was not complicated by political considerations. Crameri points to the career of Montserrat Roig who chose to write novels in Catalan but journalism in Castilian, a neat way of paying the bills.

Crameri has taken a particular interest in the position of the novelist Juan Marsé (born in 1933), who writes in Castilian, observing that although he is thought of in Spain as a whole as a Catalan, he has been disowned by the Catalan literary establishment. The truth is, he is an anti-nationalist. Marsé was adopted as a child by a couple from Barcelona, and spent his youth in the mainly Catalan-speaking Barcelona district of Gràcia. Although bilingual of speech, he has chosen to write in Castilian. Crameri has an especially interesting discussion of Marsé's *El amante bilingüe* (The Bilingual Lover), made into a film by Vicente Aranda in 1993. Crameri sees this novel as a true reflection of the city, taking into account 'the bilingual nature of its society and the mixture of cultures which influence its people.' The wife of the central character is no less than a sociolinguist working on the Language Normalisation programme, and

Crameri draws a wide but plausible significance from that fact. In the novel, as in real life, Catalonia has benefitted greatly from inward migration from other parts of Spain, and those people are as much part of its future as of its past. This sense that Catalonia's national identity is bound up with its immigrant population becomes truer every year, as people from a much wider area — North Africa, Latin America, South Asia — come to live and work in the country. Any prescriptive attempt to persuade 'Catalan' novelists to write 'Catalan' novels that ignore the linguistic and cultural complexity is doomed to failure. Quim Monzó, who has written both journalism and novels in Catalan, is as conscious as any of the pressures of Catalan literary orthodoxy, of a political correctness that can make it hard to describe the somewhat confusing reality of Catalonia, in which people chop and change between the two languages, often choosing words from one language when speaking the other.

The position in the cinema is rather more clear-cut than it is with books. As we noted in the previous chapter there is a Catalan-language film industry, and it has produced some notable films. But Miquel Strubell's chapter on the language in Keown's *Companion to Catalan Culture* suggests only 4% of all cinema-goers watch films in Catalan. Jaume Martí-Olivella in his chapter on cinema in the same volume suggests 7% watching 'Catalan films' but this may include Catalan films with a Castilian soundtrack. Additionally, many viewers now access films via DVD or the internet, so any figures should be treated with caution.

One film set in Barcelona but which uses Castilian Spanish is 'Libertarias' (1996; the English title 'Freedom Fighters' is misleading, perhaps 'Free Women' would have been better). This concerns the struggle by anarchist women in 1936–1937 to gain recognition as combatants in the republican militias, rather than as supporters of their male comrades. Two women from the militias are joined in the struggle by a nun and a prostitute who find common cause in the battle against capitalism and for women's rights. The film celebrates the history of the Spanish libertarian women's organisation Mujeres Libres (Free Women) and here the use of Castilian Spanish seems appropriate in recognising the work of an organisation which placed class conflict above nationalist concerns. Laura Manyà, who appears in 'Libertarias' had acted in the delightful comedy 'La Teta y la Luna' (Bigas Luna, 1994). The central character, Tete, is in search of the perfect breast to replace that of his mother who has just given birth to a demanding baby brother. The setting is very Catalan, Torredembarra, a beach resort near Altafulla, on the rather dull coast heading down towards Tarragona. Significantly, the film opens and ends with a scene of *castellers* (human castle-building), a popular culture activity which will be discussed in the next chapter. Tete is the *anxaneta*, the small boy or girl whose job is to climb right to the top of the castle.

Yet what Barcelona-born Bigas Luna does is to subvert any possible nationalist expectations by setting the film in a trilingual (Castilian-Catalan-French) multinational context. One particular use of Catalan is a satirical scene in which a boat-on-wheels decorated in the red and yellow stripes of the Catalan flag enters the Big Top to the music of an *habanera* and shouts of *Visca Catalunya* (Long Live Catalonia). Tete's mother is Andalusian, while his rival for the affections of Estrellita, the French singer, is the would-be flamenco singer Miguel. Estrellita's partner Maurice is Portuguese, and rides around on a Harley Davidson, so this is a pretty mongrel crew. Tete has a day-dream of planting the Catalan and European flags on the moon. Baby brother in the hospital nursery wears a *barretina* (a traditional Catalan cap), and also appears dressed in a cap at the completion of the film's final successful *castell*. Human desires are universal, the film suggests, but exist within a complex global pattern of intersecting cultures and languages. Bigas Luna described this in an interview as 'this ethnic mixture of cultures'. There is a certain irony in the fact that the internationally successful Bigas Luna died

150

in 2013 while working on a film adaptation of a Catalan novel by Manuel de Pedrolo.

2. A multilingual musical interlude

Language has been a key political issue in Greater Catalonia during the past half century. Perhaps mid-chapter is a good point to consider how far it may be an almost incidental aspect of being human at any given place or time. Antonio Muñoz Molina was born in Jaén, a small provincial capital in Andalusia, and grew up full of the desire to get away and be a citizen of the world. He challenges us to reconsider whether attachment to the local is necessarily a progressive cause: 'The Right, since German Romanticism, had celebrated the local; the Left the universal; the Right loyalty to the earth and blood; the Left, internationalism and world citizenship.' For young people in the 1960s, 'Pride in the local seemed to us to be an unmistakeable sign of stupidity'. He points out that support for the Catalans and Basques, in whatever language, was an integral part of opposition to the Franco regime: 'I can remember the first time that I heard (Raimon's) 'Al Vent' as clearly as the first time that I heard (Bob Dylan's) 'Blowin' in the Wind', with a similar shiver of clandestine rebellion.'

> Al vent,
> la cara al vent,
> el cor al vent,
> les mans al vent,
> els ulls al vent,
> al vent del món.

> *(In the wind, / face in the wind, / heart in the wind, / hands in the wind, / eyes in the wind, / in the wind of the world)*

> I tots,
> tots plens de nit,

buscant la llum,
buscant la pau,
buscant a déu,
al vent del món.

(And everyone, / everyone full of the night, / looking for the light, / looking for peace, / looking for god, / in the wind of the world)

In the same way, people in Greater Catalonia loved Paco Ibañez, and especially his version of a poem by the young goatherd-poet Miguel Hernández, born in Orihuela in the far south of the Valencian Community. A communist, Hernández fought in the war, was arrested and imprisoned after it and died in prison in Alicante from TB in 1942. He was just 32 years old, and his name is remembered in the name of one of Elche's three universities. The poem is 'Andaluces de Jaén' (Andalusians from Jaén) the birthplace of Muñoz Molina:

Andaluces de Jaén,
aceituneros altivos,
decidme en el alma: ¿quién,
quién levantó los olivos?

(Andalusians from Jaén / proud olive-growers / tell me in your heart, who / who planted the olive-trees?) Ibánez sings '¿de quién, / de quién son estos olivos? — *to whom, / to whom do the olive-trees belong?)*

Ibáñez's own biography is a reflection of a general cause that seems to have fragmented since the heady days of the 1960s. He was born in Valencia City to a Valencian father and a Basque mother. His father went into exile in 1939, and Paco fled Spain to join him in 1948, falling under the spell of the French anarchist singer Georges Brassens and participating in the 1968 revolt in Paris, singing his songs in the courtyard of the Sorbonne. Fittingly, Jaén is derived from the Arabic word for a crossing-place for caravans.

152

3. Varieties of Catalan in Valencia, North Catalonia and the Balearic Islands

The Catalan language has received enormous official support over the past thirty years in Catalonia. The situation is much patchier in the other territories of Greater Catalonia. The survival of Catalan in North Catalonia is rather more unlikely, but owes a lot to the relative isolation of this small corner of the French Republic. Until recently it had received little official support, but this is now changing. *'Perpinyà la Catalana'* is not just an advertising slogan to attract tourists: Catalan is still the language of many street conversations, Catalan flags are everywhere, and many streets display their names in the language. While Catalan is not an official language it is recognised as a 'regional language' which qualifies it for support in the fields of education and media.

The teaching of the language in schools in North Catalonia is crucial to its survival there: whereas most older people speak Catalan, only a small minority of young people do so. A combination of official and voluntary effort has given the language a toe-hold in nursery and primary education, but in secondary education, Catalan is not offered as a 'first' foreign language which would give it compulsory status, and much is down to individual schools. The University of Perpignan offers Catalan Studies, and this has enabled young people from universities in South Catalonia, Valencia and the Balearic Islands to study there under the European Union Erasmus schemes. Such schemes are important in maintaining links between the two territories. There are few Catalan print media outlets in France, but the outlook is rather better with radio and television, because the regional government and EU grants finance relays which enable people in North Catalonia to receive radio and TV broadcasts from south of the border. However, precisely because they are coming from across the border many of the programmes are of limited interest to people living in France.

In the other territories of Greater Catalonia, language policies in education reflect the fact that Catalan — and its Valencian, Mallorcan, Menorcan and Ibizan variants — is the first language of many or most of the inhabitants. In Catalonia, Catalan has always been seen as the language of social and economic power, and thus as a desirable language in which to achieve fluency. The position is rather different in Valencian and the Balearic Islands, where Catalan tended to be seen as the language of rural peasants, while Castilian was the language of powerful, urban dwellers, trade and industry, print, radio and television. Joan Fuster, writing in the middle of the twentieth century and at a time when it was sensible not to be too frank about linguistic politics, observed the complications arising from the existence of considerable areas where Castilian rather than Valencian had always been the first language.

Since that time, the arrival of Castilian-speaking migrants has added to the complications, together with people moving from Northern Europe who tend to acquire some Castilian rather than Valencian as their 'local' language. As Valencia expanded to become a grand and splendid European city, the tightly-packed areas which had always been a stronghold of the Valencian language were thinned out or emptied with people moving out to the suburbs. The area within the old city walls had a population of 30,000 in 2012 compared with five times that figure one hundred years previously. To celebrate the 50th anniversary of Fuster's *Nosaltres, els Valencians*, Vicent Sanchis in his 2012 book *Valencians Encara* (Still Valencians) pointed out the falseness of claims of bilingualism in the Valencian Community. For him the truth was that only Valencian-speaking areas were bilingual, since in Castilian-speaking areas that was generally the only language used. It is for this reason that the Valencian language has tended to be a divisive political issue with only some of its supporters tending to favour reintegration into Greater Catalonia (the *Països Catalans*, PPCC, project) while others recognise it as proof of a separate Valencian identity.

Carme Miquel, a teacher and leading supporter of the language, has added to our knowledge of bilingualism in the Valencian Community in a delightful book addressed to her daughter, *A Cau d'Orella* (A Word in your Ear). After the Civil War, middle-class people in Valencia and other big towns such as Xativa changed to Castilian, while in Alicante it happened earlier, and Castellon remained mainly Valencian. But in Valencia City, 'To speak Valencian marked you out as a villager, ignorant, end of story'. If the political project of Greater Catalonia receives limited support in the Valencian Community, the educational use of the language as a demonstration of a valued local culture gains a much higher degree of support. More than 50% of children in the Valencian Community choose the 'Valencian line' at school, or have it chosen for them by their parents. This means that the normal language of education is Valencian, with Spanish as a second language. In the Castilian line, Valencian adopts a similar subaltern position. In the playground, children seem much more relaxed about the language issue, with continual movement from one language to the other, no doubt mixing up the two languages in ways that might shock their teachers. However, the Council of Europe has criticised the Generalitat Valenciana on a number of occasions for failing to meet the demand for Valencian-language education.

Schools are the responsibility of the autonomous governments in Spain. The Spanish government passed a law (the Wert Law, after the name of the education minister) in 2014 which insists that every student has the right to be taught in Castilian if he or she demands it, but it is not clear what if any effect this will have in Catalonia. Since most of the opposition parties in the Spanish parliament are committed to repealing this law if the Popular Party loses power, autonomous governments are in no hurry to implement it. If the Valencian Community has tended to resist Catalan by dragging its feet, the government of the Balearic Islands attempted to introduce a new law governing the use of language in education. In brief, the new law would have replaced a bilingual system by a tri-lingual system, whereby some subjects at primary and secondary level would be taught in English, thus effectively reducing the amount of teaching in Catalan. The proposal led to massive demonstrations — 80,000 people in Palma gathered in Mallorca's biggest ever public demonstration in the autumn of 2013 — and there were school strikes lasting three weeks supported by teachers and students in towns throughout the islands. Opposition was based partly on the principle of the new law but also on the practical question of whether there would be sufficient qualified teachers to carry through such a reform. Official statistics showed that the percentages of students choosing Catalan-medium education in 2014 were 75% in Mallorca (the largest and most populated island), 66% in Menorca, 42% in Ibiza and 61% in Formentera. And in 2014 to complicate matters still further, the High Court in Palma declared the new tri-lingual law, well, unlawful. With the Popular Party losing control of the autonomous governments of Valencia and the Balearic Islands in 2015, the outcome of these various reforms and debates is uncertain. But education seems destined to continue to be a political battle-ground in the future. Which is not really the purpose of education, is it?

As for the press, it must always be taken into account that newspaper readership is less common in all parts of Spain than in the UK. Newspapers depend on readers forming fixed habits, and those Catalans who bought newspapers continue in the main to buy Castilian language papers. The spectacular breakthrough came towards the end of 1997 when the popular daily *El Periódico* decided to produce a Catalan language edition in addition to its Castilian edition. The following year it accounted for 50% of total sales in Catalan, and had pushed the percentage of paper sales in Catalan up to the 25% mark. Outside of Barcelona, there are lively local papers in Catalan as well, noticeably *El Punt*, the Gerona daily, which has not only managed to steadily increase its sales over the years, but has also spawned editions in other Catalan towns such as Tortosa, and weekly editions in North Catalonia and Valencia.

In relation to media output in Catalan, the general point is that digital technology has opened up new possibilities for Catalan language broadcasting at a local level, but that in the main such opportunities have been taken up by companies with no roots in Greater Catalonia and who are unsympathetic to the language and culture. Rafael Xambó's comment about Valencia, that in television there has been a race to the bottom among both private and public sector broadcasters, with schedules dominated by banal entertainment, is unfortunately true of Catalonia and the Balearic Islands as well. TV3 is the channel financed by and substantially controlled by the Catalan Generalitat. For some time this was also available in other parts of Greater Catalonia, but as the Valencian Generalitat and the Balearic government developed their own autonomous TV stations (Channel 9 and IB3) they also moved to block reception of TV3. This means that viewers in Barcelona can watch IB3 and Channel 9 but not vice-versa. In Catalonia, TV3's audience share fell from 21% in 2000 to 14% in 2010 largely because of the introduction of new digital channels. Xambó notes continuing political interference both at the level of who has concessions to broadcast and also with content. For example, IB3 is unable to broadcast material critical of the Balearic government. During the Transition period in the 1970s, the Spanish national television service (TVE) in Valencia included a half-hour of news in Catalan, which dealt robustly with what Xambó calls 'the conflicts and the problems of the Valencian reality', including the Valencian language. However, given the divisive and at times violent nature of Valencian politics, this proved controversial. The producer and other staff received personal threats during the 'Battle of Valencia', the same period when Fuster's home was bombed in 1978 and 1981.

In recent years, TV3 has proved controversial for what is seen by the political opponents of Catalan nationalism as its open support for the nationalist cause. In particular, the political satire show 'Polònia' (Poland) has aroused much criticism. Such shows are uncommon anywhere in Spain, and since it was launched in 2006 the show has generated a large following. Its title derived from the derogatory use of the term 'Poles' by Spaniards to describe the Catalans. Actors mimic leading political figures, who change according to the ups and downs of politics and the issues of the day. The treatment of President Mas was especially effective during the campaign leading up to the independence vote in 2014, with his character unable to say the word 'independence' in public, while privately dreaming about it. It is his colleagues who point out to him that it is not going to happen magically, but only if he commits to the idea of independence and works actively to make it happen. While politicians of all parties are treated critically, there is little doubt, according to Kathryn Crameri, that Popular Party leaders come in for especially strong criticism of both their actions and their motives.

4. The current status of Catalan

From an English perspective, all this fuss about language and languages may seem a storm in a teacup. In an increasingly interdependent world, in which English is rapidly gaining ground as an international language, is it not illogical to be worrying about the future of less-spoken languages? Bearing in mind that the vast majority of Catalan speakers (with the exception of North Catalonia and the Sardinian enclave of Alghero) also speak Spanish, one of the great world languages, why should they also bother with a local language? Such questions can be answered in three ways, firstly with specific reference to Catalan as a 'big' language in Europe, secondly in relation to politics and culture, and thirdly in relation to the localism which is now seen increasingly as the other face of globalisation.

By European standards, Catalan is not a small language. It has more speakers than Finnish, Danish or Norwegian and nearly as many as countries such as Greece and Portugal. The confusion is not so much about numbers of speakers as about the common sense notion that there should be some kind of match between language and nation. Yet this is clearly not the case. French is not just the language of France, but has official status in Belgium, Luxembourg and Switzerland. Finnish is the majority language of Finland but there is a substantial Swedish-speaking minority with its own schools, university and Members of Parliament. In the far north, Sami is a completely distinct language spoken by traditionally nomadic people who roam from Norway across Sweden and Finland to Russia. Finnish, Sami and Swedish are all mutually unintelligible. One of the many problems of Catalan is that it is not sufficiently differentiated from neighbouring languages including not only Castilian, but also the various dialects/languages of Southern France. As far as the European Union is concerned, Catalan finds itself refused official status within European organisations and lumped together with all the other officially small and deserving languages, that is, those languages that are not readily identified as national languages. These include 58,000 speakers of Scots Gaelic and the 300 people who speak Livonian, a language spoken in Latvia, the last native speaker of which died in 2013. A language, you might say, needs a nation, and a nation needs a state. There is the rub for the ten million Catalan-speakers.

Politics and culture can offer the opportunity for a language to flourish, yet it is obvious that languages can survive under very harsh conditions indeed. Slovene, for example, that finally emerged in 1991 as the language of an independent country, Slovenia, which is now a member of the European Union, survived for many centuries as a local language always under the dominations of outsiders, whether the Venetians, the Hapsburg Empire, or twentieth century Yugoslavia. Its use as a literary language was somewhat sporadic, even more so than in the case of Catalan, but Slovene remained the language of folk-tales and folk-music, and the particular material cultures of its people in the harsh foothills of the Alps, the lush countryside around Ljubljana or the Adriatic coastline. An additional point of interest is that even in a small country like Slovenia, there are national minorities speaking Italian and Hungarian whose rights are defined and defended within the Slovene constitution.

Within the medieval kingdom of Aragon, Catalan flourished by contrast as a language of power, spreading to Valencia and the islands by conquest. Its success is an extraordinary contrast with Aragonese, now spoken by only a few thousand people in Huesca province. Alongside political power, it also flourished as a language of literary and intellectual life, most notably in the work of Raymond Lully. Having survived some centuries of decline as a language of power, Catalan was revived in the nineteenth century to become a major language of literature and politics in the twentieth century. It is also worth noting that it survived as a language of popular culture, a subject we shall be considering in some detail in the next chapter.

The third set of reasons for taking the Catalan language seriously are in some ways more fundamental than arguments about what constitutes a 'big' or 'small' language, or about the interpenetration of language and power. We now recognise biodiversity as a key issue in the survival of life on earth, as we see plant and animal species disappearing in the face of the onslaught from urbanisation, industrialisation, money-grabbing capitalists and the sheer predatory weight of human beings *vis-à-vis* the rest of life on earth. Increasingly, human beings have begun to realise the folly of their ways and the importance of defending biodiversity at every turn. Globalisation, with its vast inter-continental movement of goods, services and people, and instant telecommunications, is viewed increasingly not as a way to further understanding between the peoples of the world but as a concerted attempt to wipe out local differences of customs, belief, culture and language. In other words, the same forces that threaten biodiversity in the physical world threaten the viability of local languages and cultures.

Anyone who had the pleasure of hearing Rhodri Morgan happily fielding First Minister's questions in both Welsh and English at the new National Assembly in Cardiff will have recognised with respect the vigour of a language and culture which for 900 years has refused to die in the face of English expansionism. Equally those who respect a plurality of languages may have been disappointed to hear members of the Catalan and Valencian parliaments hurling abuse at one another, or appalled to hear the lack of respect for the rights of the people of Catalonia dripping from the mouths of Madrid politicians who seem to have learned very little from the debacles of twentieth century Spanish history. Languages and cultures, like nations, should be 'a legacy and an undertaking' to repeat the words of Joan Maragall, our mother and our child.

Chapter 7
Culture, Popular Culture and Everyday Life

*Excesses — real excesses, let us not deceive ourselves —
are the only things that brighten up life.*

1. The cultures of Greater Catalonia

Young people growing up in Greater Catalonia have access to a greater number of 'cultures' than any generation in history. There is the 'high' culture of classical music, opera houses, art galleries and museums. There is the international pop culture of rock music, Disney and Bond films, and the 'banal entertainment' of television. There are the cultures of various ethnic minority groups who have settled in these lands in recent years. And then there is what will emerge as the subject matter of this chapter, the popular culture of locality, the festivities, often with folkloric overlays, which animate life in small towns and villages throughout the area. Of course, these categories overlap. So 'going to the cinema' or 'watching a DVD' in Barcelona, Palma and Valencia can vary between an art-house film in almost any world language including Catalan at one extreme to watching the latest English-language Hollywood block-buster dubbed into Castilian Spanish at the other. The same people can dip into a number of different kinds of culture during the week, watching the local football club play at the weekend, going to a pop or classical music concert one evening, relaxing on the sofa with a Disney film, and turning out for the village *festa (fiesta)* which may include dodgem car-rides alongside a display of *castellers* (human castle-building), or the dancing of *sardanas* (the ancient and emblematic Catalan circle-dance) alongside an all-night disco. Needless to say there will be food and drink and music weaving their way riotously among whatever activities are taking place. Popular culture is about excess, as Joan Fuster rightly pointed out, and it was so even in the rather quieter days of the old dictator.

High culture has become something of a bidding war in recent years, as towns and cities strive to outdo one another for the most exotic, most expensive, most *avant garde* cultural venues. Culture is seen as part of competitive advantage as cities seek to outbid one another for footloose global capital, factories, offices and warehouses. England has not been immune to this, as any visitor to Newcastle/Gateshead (the Sage Gateshead and the Baltic Centre for Contemporary Art) or Manchester (Bridgewater Hall) will be aware. In Greater Catalonia, high culture has been seen as a way of reviving run-down areas of big cities, attracting wealthy tourists and adding to the prestige of local politicians. It is as well to be aware of this before proceeding to the more modest ambitions of popular culture. High culture tends towards the grandiose in both the Valencian Community and in Catalonia.

In Valencia, the largest and noisiest site is without doubt the City of Arts and Sciences, begun in 1994 and finished in 2005. The chief architect was Valencia's own son Santiago Calatrava, and the political impetus was provided by the socialists who were running the Generalitat Valenciana at that time. No doubt if the term 'white elephant' existed in Valencian, the opposition Popular Party would have called it that; instead they described it as the 'work of the Pharaohs' because of the scale and size and expense of the project. To enter its portals is to be aware of the many ironies of modern

Spain: the competitive desire of autonomous communities to score points against their neighbours, the magnitude of the financial expenditure and the consequent indebtedness of government, and finally the sheer amount of fun that it is possible to have during a day out at the City of Arts and Sciences. Whether your cultural interests are stimulated by the planetarium of L'Hemisfèric, with its shutters imitating the opening and closing of the human eye, the Science Museum, the landscaped walks and sculptures of L'Umbracle, the Aquarium, the Opera House (Palau de les Arts Reina Sofia) or the open-air concert arena named L'Àgora in conscious imitation of the Roman past, there is amusement galore at the City of Arts and Sciences. It is all rather overwhelming, but it is always possible to retire for dinner to one of the restaurants of the award-winning Veles i Vents building built to house the crews competing in the 2007 America's Cup sailing race, an event which Valencia pipped both Palma and Barcelona for the prestige of hosting, in itself a satisfaction to local pride.

Castellon is often regarded as the white elephant capital of the Valencian Community. It is home to an airport completed in 2011 at a cost of £130 million which at the time of writing (2015) is yet to receive an aircraft. Every few months, optimistic press stories appear announcing its imminent opening for traffic but so far nothing has happened. Meanwhile tax-payers are making interest payments for the cost for a facility that is neither providing a service nor rendering an income. The Cultural Castellon project is another rather inflated plan that has come to fruition, providing a building that houses a concert hall, two further halls and exhibition and entertainment spaces in the city. One of these spaces is called the Magic Box (which appears to host mainly rock bands and discos), and one wonders by what magic a town of less than 200,000 population and an unemployment rate of over one quarter is ever going to make full use of these splendid facilities, especially since Castellon has a fine late nineteenth century theatre which has been renovated and has been the usual location for both plays and concerts in the past.

Barcelona has also invested heavily in cultural infrastructure. Some of the best work here has been in remodelling older buildings. Thus the Olympic Stadium for the 1992 Olympic Games is the stadium built at Montjuïc forthe 1929 Exhibition and used the 1936 Workers' Olympiad in opposition to that year's Berlin Olympics. The remodelled National Palace is now a worthy home for the Catalan Art Museum, with its valuable collection of Romanesque murals from the early medieval Pyrenean churches. As if to make an architectural history point, the classical Palace stands next door to one of the iconic buildings of twenty-first century Modernism, Mies van der Rohe's German Pavilion from the 1929 Exhibition, now happily rebuilt here at Montjuïc. Just across the road, the fine *Art Nouveau* Ramona textile factory has become one of Barcelona's most popular and prestigious exhibition spaces, the CaixaForum with a fine, understated underground entrance with bookshop, cloakrooms, meeting rooms and reception areas by the Japanese architect Arata Isozaki. The *Modernista* Palace of Catalan Music (the Palau) has also been refurbished to meet twentieth century performance standards.

So far, so good, but not to be outdone by its Valencian neighbours, Barcelona then launched into further new building projects, including the new National Theatre, and a new concert hall (the Auditori) which incorporates a music museum. MACBA, Barcelona's Contemporary Art Museum, is a vast building erected as part of the overall redevelopment of the area known as the Raval on the right-hand side of the Rambla (or Ramblas) descending towards the sea, an area traditionally associated with prostitution and drugs. It can be an intimidating place to visit with small numbers of visitors often overwhelmed by the size and scale of the exhibits. I am sure most art-lovers visiting Barcelona would prefer the medieval palaces of the Picasso Museum or the modernist cool of Josep Lluís Sert's Miró foundation at Montjuïc.

The white elephants of high culture do not seem to be quite the excesses to which Fuster was referring. Popular culture, the local and traditional, has pursued a rather more economical route but seems to hold a much firmer place in the hearts of the inhabitants of Greater Catalonia and the appreciation of visitors. One tradition maintained throughout Greater Catalonia is choral singing, and perhaps more than any other activity these choirs form a link between classical and popular, past and present, tradition and innovation. The Palau (Palace of Catalan Music) in Barcelona is a good place to start. Its founders would be very surprised to learn that is now a World Heritage site. It is a masterpiece by Lluís Domènech i Muntaner, less well known perhaps than Gaudí, but a major exponent of *Modernisme*, especially as applied to public buildings (his other masterpiece in Barcelona is the Sant Pau hospital). The Palau building shimmers with light reflected from coloured tiles, stained glass and polished wood. It is the only concert-hall in Europe that needs no artificial lighting during daylight hours.

This extraordinary building was erected as the headquarters of a choir — the Orfeó Català — which explains why it is one of the few *Modernista* buildings in the old town. The choir wanted it to be within walking distance of their working-class membership, rather than in the new town of the nineteenth century middle-class extension (L'Eixample), where most *Modernista* buildings are to be found. The 2,000 seats reflected the number of members of the society at that point. The Orfeó, established in 1892, has always sung classical choral works, but its repertoire has also included choral settings of old Catalan songs and ballads, precisely the range established in the 1860s by Josep Anselm Clavé and the many choirs he established around the country, including the

Valencian Community. Thus choral singing was an integral part of the Catalan *Renaixença* (Renaissance) movement of the mid-nineteenth century, a movement which also impacted on the cultural life of Valencia and the Balearic Islands. Nowadays, choirs in Greater Catalonia sing a wide range of music, for music has that unique virtue of linking one culture with another in a way that is much more difficult for cultural media dependent on the spoken or written word. I recall a warm autumn evening in the not so distant past on a balcony in Ciutadella (Menorca) listening to a local choir rehearsing in a community centre a few doors away. Mixed with traditional Menorcan songs was a whole modern repertoire of familiar songs in English.

The outbreak of the Civil War interrupted rehearsals for a performance of Beethoven's Ninth Symphony at the Palau. It was meant to celebrate world peace, alongside the celebration of the alternative 1936 Workers' Olympiad in Barcelona. The conductor was Pau (Pablo) Casals, who at the end of the Civil War was to take himself and his music-making into exile. He was rehearsing Beethoven's Ninth on 18 July 1936 when news of the military rebellion came through. As Colm Tóibín tells it in *Homage to Barcelona*, 'Casals and his orchestra were advised to go home as quickly as they could. They had completed the first three movements of the symphony, and Casals asked the musicians and singers if they would finish it. They agreed.' Thirty-four years later in the Palau, 5 June 1970, I heard Helen Watts and Gerald English, three Catalan choral societies and the Barcelona Orchestra perform the same symphony to rapturous applause. It was an 'I was there' moment.

Popular folk culture is linked closely to the seasons and agricultural life, and this seems a good starting-point to choose. Popular culture in England, apart from rare survivals, is almost entirely the product of the past two centuries (spectator sports, TV and radio, and the popular press). This is not the case in Greater Catalonia, where industrialisation came much later, if at all. People who have migrated to the great cities are also more likely to retain links with their native village and go back for local holidays and celebrations. But it is more than just differences in the pace of economic and social change. A popular national culture survived, or in many cases was reinvented, precisely because of the determined attempt to destroy it. In Catalonia especially, a number of cultural forms emerged, or re-emerged, with specific nationalist meanings. These included forms as different as the *sardana*, the origins of which are lost in Mediterranean antiquity, and the *habanera* song and dance music imported into the coastal towns of Catalonia by colonial trade, music which fused Andalusian and African influences. The *sardana* became linked to a particular wind band called the *cobla*. In the *sardana*, the band remains seated, but for any events requiring movement the key instruments are the *gralla* (shawm), the *flabiol* (a kind of piccolo that can be played one-handed) and the *tamborí* (small drum). These are ideal for use in processions, and for *castellers* displays, but very different from the larger marching bands for which Valencia is famous.

The winter season, as throughout Europe and beyond, is the season of light festivals which have become inextricably mixed up with the Christian celebrations of Christmas. Christmas markets, Christmas trees and illuminated decorations are found in every city in Greater Catalonia, but there are also variations which make each celebration slightly different. There is little doubt that January 6 is the Big Day for children, because that is when the Three Kings (Three Wise Men) bring the children their presents. In Valencia the Kings parade with decorated floats on January 5, distributing sweets to all and sundry as a warm-up to the big day. In Ibiza Town, the Kings cross the harbour in a lighted barge before parading through the town on horseback. In Barcelona they arrive each year from the sea in their splendid robes and proceed to take presents to children in hospitals and orphanages before settling down to a splendid feast. Barcelona also celebrates Saint Lucy (December 13), whose name is also attached to the colourful Barcelona Christmas market in front of the cathedral. In rural Catalonia there are popular celebrations that give priority to Christmas Day and Saint Nicholas (December 6). For St Nicholas, children wassail their neighbours carrying wicker baskets which they hope their neighbours will fill with treats such as fruit and nuts, and go from house to house singing traditional St Nicholas songs. Boy bishops are chosen at religious houses such as Montserrat, and this custom is celebrated in Palma de Mallorca too. St Nicholas is the patron saint of Alicante, and here his day is celebrated in flamboyant fashion with a great procession animated by marching bands.

Traditional festivities which coincide with the Christian period of Lent are broadly related to crop-sowing and to various beliefs about the driving out of evil spirits and the need for renewal. There is too the old belief that some sort of sacrifice is necessary in order to secure renewed fertility. At Canals in the Valencian Community, a huge bonfire is built in the main square and burned on January 16. It is thatched with green pine boughs and topped incongruously by a small orange tree. But it is *Carnaval* which is the major event. A 'carnival' in many countries has become simply a generic term for any public merry-making involving processions and music and dancing, but throughout the Hispanic and Luso-Brazilian world, it remains firmly anchored to the last few days in February or early March before Lent begins. It has been a longstanding cause of dispute between church, state, and civil society. In Catalonia it includes, for example, the character of the King of Fools, or Lord of Misrule, who preaches a 'sermon' to the people which usually consists of a satirical attack on local political leaders. *Carnaval* is celebrated in many towns in the Valencian Community, but in Valencia City, it takes second place to the extraordinary festival of the *Falles* described below. Yet the burning of the floats at the end of the *Falles* serves the same symbolic function of sacrifice and renewal as the mock solemn burial of the Lord of Misrule in traditional *Carnaval* festivities.

Easter is a key time of rebirth and growth in which the pagan and the Christian have become hopelessly entwined. Throughout Greater Catalonia, the streets are crowded with processions carrying white palm, and this ceremony is especially important in Elche, where they cut fresh palm leaves from Europe's only natural palm-grove. Yet this ceremony has very ancient roots deeper than those of the Catholic Church. In Greece and Rome about this time there were festivals dedicated to the laurel and the olive. The olive and its oil were basic to the economy and therefore the culture of the Mediterranean world. The olive tree lived to an incredible age, by the measurement of a single human life. The laurel was much used in cooking in the form of bay leaves, and was reputed to have magic properties in warding off lightning, as well as being associated with the god Jupiter. A crown of laurel leaves was the classical symbol of victory, and the palm branches carried across the shoulder have become the laurel of Palm Sunday in the commemoration of Christ's triumphal entry into Jerusalem.

After Easter comes the cycle of the tree and the rose, the ancient Roman Floral Games. This is reflected in Catalonia in a number of traditions. The roses offered to the loved one on St George's Day (April 23) is the most obvious one, but there are also maypole celebrations in various parts of Catalonia, while floral carpets are laid in Sitges and Gerona. But the most vivid and popular celebrations are those that have become attached to Corpus Christi, two months after Easter. Corpus was an explicit attempt in medieval Europe, by Pope John XXII in 1320 to be precise, to provide a Christian alternative to pagan rituals associated with springtime. Robert Hughes' fine book *Barcelona* describes how the pavements of the streets would be strewn with 'flowering broom, thyme, rosemary, carnations, and rose petals' before the processions started. Processions featured figures familiar to modern popular culture such as dragons, giants and devils. Corpus in Palma de Mallorca is still a medley of the Christian and pagan, with floral carpets laid in front of the cathedral and a religious procession after mass including folk elements such as the dancing horse figures and the dancers *(cossiers)* who clutch handfuls of greenery and flowers. In some Mallorcan communities, the *cossiers* even dance inside the village church. The floral theme is continued into summer in Valencia with the famous battle of the flowers.

While midsummer does not have quite the same meaning it has in the Nordic countries, it is nevertheless an excuse for yet more noisy parties. In another of those familiar Christian-pagan amalgams, it has become closely associated with St John's Day, and so the main party is on St John's Eve, 23 June, when bonfires and fireworks are lit throughout Greater Catalonia. Fireworks continue pretty much through the summer, when most villages celebrate their *festa major* (main festival) which has its origin in harvest festivities. Indeed, in some inland villages where the main crop is the olive, the *festa major* takes place in the winter when the olives are shaken down from the trees. The two most traditional Catalan folk festivities symbolise the collective endeavour needed for a successful harvest. These are the *sardana* and the *castellers*, the human castle builders, both of which were revived during the nineteenth century. To some extent, the importance of the *festa major* has been overtaken in the Valencian Community by the Moors and Christians festivities which have a historical origin in the medieval conflicts between Al-Andalus and the Christian kingdoms of Castile and Aragon and are described below.

2. Popular culture on the Balearic Islands

Amy Baumann (writing as Alexis Brown) lived in rural Ibiza in the 1960s and wrote about popular celebrations in her enchanting memoir *A Valley Wide*. In a chapter titled 'Old Customs, New Cast' she describes the impact of 'modern industrial civilisation' on a traditional rural community which had changed little since 'biblical times', as the new road that would link their village to the rest of the island came ever closer. She describes her children joining in the local celebrations of St John's Eve (Midsummer) putting together the traditional bonfire: 'Green wood boiled with sappy hisses and sighs, pluming purple smoke above the orange flame.' As the fireworks fizz and the rockets whizz they identify the fires burning at other farms in the valley. Yet the tradition was dying, not least because of the difficulties in Franco's days of getting permission for such celebrations. José, a neighbour, comments: "Now I come up here to see you foreigners keep the old traditions." Amy Baumann was right that the old way of life was coming to a close, and yet wrong as well, because in the new democratic Ibiza, both locals and incomers have worked to revive the old ways, and Saint John's Eve is now as great a celebration on the island as it has ever been. Peasants may have become wealthy business people, the island may be at times in danger of being overwhelmed by partying tourists, and yet something of the old relationship between people and nature, the old magic, has survived.

Saint John's Eve is also celebrated on Mallorca, including the superstition that a bathe at sunrise on June 24 will keep you healthy for the following year. Jacqueline Waldren, a long-time resident, noted in her study of the island *Insiders and Outsiders* that people from the village of Deià living and working in other parts of the island, or even in France, would make a special effort to be in the village for St John's Eve celebrations.

She observed very precisely how the continuing celebration of tradition kept together a community which otherwise might have little in common. 'These traditional practices', she wrote, 'which are an effective means for preserving a sense of continuity, also create a convenient façade behind which all kinds of new and different relationships, beliefs, morals, and values are absorbed. People have learned to maintain tradition selectively. That which fits needs is perpetuated and that which does not is forgotten and not mentioned.'

A good example of this selective approach to tradition is the evolution of local village *festes* on Mallorca. Tomás Graves, brought up at Deià and to all intents and purposes a Mallorcan, comments on this in his musical memoir *Tuning up at Dawn*. As a musician himself, he notes how debased these occasions had become culturally, with vapid dance-music, 'stale folk dance routines' and bedroom farces. Into this Graves and his Mallorcan friends inserted both rock music and the politicised Catalan singing known as the *nova cançó*. Two of the best of these singers, Maria del Mar Bonet and Guillem d'Efak were Mallorcan, but had made their names in Barcelona, singing in clubs and theatres. The success of Graves was to introduce this kind of music back into village square festivities.

Popular culture in the Balearics faces a lot of competition, and rather than adopt an exclusive approach, it has succeeded well where it has reached out to meet the modern world in a way that has wider relevance to these societies. Waldren mentions a man she heard speaking at a public meeting in Deià, who had spent fifty years working in France: "Men from Deià were forced to emigrate to South America, the United States and later to France. Many never came 'home' and others like myself managed to return only for our final years. To us, 'coming home' means participating, helping the village to maintain itself and grow. Foreigners can stay, they should stay (and) help us today, not by idealising our past which may seem pleasing to them but was oppressive to us, but by taking an active part in securing our young people's future.' Education, music, jobs, holding closely to what is distinctive and different about their way of life, but prepared to meet the modern world head on.

Graves emphasises in both his writing about music, and about local food cultures (*Bread and Oil: Majorcan Culture's Last Stand*) the cleavage between Mallorca and Menorca despite the fact that one island is clearly visible from the other. 'I've visited Minorca (sic) seven times, about six more than the average Majorcan (sic) of my age.' Thus it is unsurprising that Menorcan popular culture has developed its own distinctive forms, not least in the central role of horses and riders in local festivities. These probably date back to the conquest of Menorca by Alfons III in 1287, and the replacement of the Muslim population by a Christian one organised on feudal lines. Over the centuries the horsemen who participate in Menorcan festivals, usually beginning with St John's Eve in June and spreading through the summer season until September, have come to represent in their elaborate costumes the various levels of that medieval society: nobles, clergy, merchants, tradesmen organised in their various guilds, and peasants. Each representative figure is known as a *caixer* while other characters have specific functions, such as the musician (*fabioler*) who leads and animates the processions and the figure of St John (*S'Homo d'es Be*, introduced only in the nineteenth century), dressed in fleeces and carrying a lamb. In the modern version of the festival, horses are trained to perform dressage to the beat of traditional island songs. And of course there are bonfires and fireworks, for this is after all midsummer.

A broader view of what popular culture has come to mean today on Menorca can best be gauged by attending one of the small town events, such as that at Sant Lluís, held over two weeks in late August/early September. This includes choral groups, Disney characters, football matches, swimming races, horses (of course), three giants, street parties, decorated floats and fireworks. The second weekend is dedicated especially to events for children, and the whole has the feel of a community arts festival which also manages to include traditional elements including a *fabioler* and the *caixers*. Riders and giants from other villages on the island are invited so this is by no means an exclusive *festa*.

3. The Valencian Community celebrates

Popular culture in the Valencian Community is all about local pride. In one town during the Civil War, the story goes that the two rival marching bands decided to join together because of the shortage of musicians. This was a resounding failure: even in the circumstances of war, animosity between the two groups made it impossible to find common cause. There is no doubt that the main celebrations throughout the region are those related to Moors and Christians festivals. In the *Poem of El Cid*, one of the earliest works of Castilian literature, working up an earlier oral tradition, the phrase 'moros e cristianos' is used time and again to simply mean 'everyone'. This must be our starting-point. Yet clearly, what is being celebrated is not *convivència* but the expulsion of the Muslims from Spain, the end of the great civilisation of Al-Andalus and eventually the forced conversion of those remaining. A further complicating factor that has come to the fore in our own century is that most towns and villages in the Valencian Community now have a North African Muslim population again, and that community relations are often strained.

Moors and Christians festivities are organised on the basis of clubs which represent a particular faction in the symbolic struggle between Christianity and Islam. Events are normally spread over a couple of days, with the Moors winning on Day One and the Christians on

Day Two, though as long as the Christians win eventually, the length of the event is immaterial. Such festivities are now found in many towns in the region, and on Mallorca too, but it is worth pausing a moment to track their history. Alcoy has always been considered the model for Moors and Christians, and the celebrations for some centuries had a clear religious purpose. According to the historian Burns, al-Azraq was a Muslim leader in the revolt of 1275/76, operating in the mountainous area behind Denia. He notes that 'In Valencian folklore al-Azraq lives on as a bogeyman to threaten naughty children, his name transmogrified into 'dragon': "El Drac will get you!" Mention a dragon, and can Saint George be far behind? Indeed not, and so Saint George, patron saint of Catalonia and countless other places, is drawn in as the saviour of the town because of his dragon-killing prowess. From the late eighteenth century, civil society becomes involved, and groups form. Each side has its chief, and contains fourteen groups. On the Christian side they include Basques, Andalusians and Asturians, and on the Muslim side Mudejars, Berbers and Marrakesh. Each group will have its own musical accompaniment, and as these festivities have spread, bands are increasingly borrowed from neighbouring towns and villages. A particular feature of Alcoy celebrations is the castle erected in the main square, once of wood, now of metal, which is supposed to add a realistic element to the proceedings.

The scale of public involvement is astonishing. In Castalla the festivities spread over four days, with 2,000 people (one fifth of the population) organised into seven clubs (*comparses*): Sailors, Peasants, Pirates and Christians on the Christian side, which wins on Day Four and Golden Moors, Old Moors and Mudejars opposing them, with their victory coming on Day Two. Some groups are much older than others, so the Moros Grocs (Golden Moors) celebrated their 150th anniversary in 2008. Each *comparsa* has its own musical accompaniment. The best that can be said of the costumes is that they are extremely colourful, though they do not seem to bear much relation to what either Muslims or Christians might have worn 800 years ago. Some of the scanty costumes of the Moorish women seem more suitable for some Hollywood imagining of what might be worn in the Sultan's harem.

There are a lot of ancillary activities such as choosing the 'queen': each *comparsa* has its own queen and from them the overall queen for that year is chosen. Apart from the ritual confrontations between the two sides, there are also processions, dancing and children's processions. In the lavish year books produced in Castalla for Moors and Christians, the introductory remarks from the Mayor are in Valencian, but from then on the publication is bilingual Valencian/Castilian, adding further to its size. There are historical sections with photos, and some serious articles of local interest, for example the history of medicine, local history, geology. There are also pages reflecting other local activities such as sports clubs, charities, blood donors, bands, cycling, and dance groups, including some relating to the local villages of Onil, Tibi, Xixona and Ibi. Advertising by local firms is extensive, with no-one wanting to be seen to not support the event.

There is little doubt about the colour, noise and excitement of Moors and Cristians, and the contribution these festivals make to social life and social cohesion, yet there are also doubts, particularly related to the obvious presence of migrant workers from the Maghreb in these towns and villages. These contemporary Muslims must feel very uncomfortable as they watch (if they watch) historic Muslims who every year manage to lose out, however bravely they fight. After the scandal about the portrayal of the prophet Mohammed in a Danish comic, decisions were made to drop specific religious references, such as the burning or exploding of effigies of the Prophet. The Spanish Federation of Islamic Religious Entities (FEERI) has called for the abolition of these festivities, although the regional branch of this organisation chose to separate itself from this decision, no doubt conscious of how much scope it offered to whatever anti-Muslim sentiment might already exist in the Valencian Community. On Mallorca, Moors and Christians does little for community relations either, as it celebrates not the conquest of Mallorca by the Catalans, but large, organised raids by North African pirates on the island — Pollença (Pollensa, 1550), Sóller (1561) and Andratx (1578). As in Valencia, celebrations always end in defeat for the Muslims, though at least these parties have the virtue of reminding islanders of the important historical role of women in the defence of their villages.

Two other contrasting local festivals in the Valencian community are worth singling out from the many that take place each year. The *Tomatina* tomato-fight in Buñol, just east of Valencia City, is the ultimate example of what Fuster means by excess. The history is more interesting in many ways than the event itself. It all began when a young participant in a Giants and Big Heads procession in the 1940s fell off a float, starting a fight which upset a market stall and led to the youngsters pelting one another with ripe tomatoes. At various times during the Franco regime, the tomato-fight was banned as a public nuisance (which it probably is). The authorities even tried locking up participants, but by 1957 the event had sufficient public support for it to become official, albeit with a few rules limiting the duration of the battle and requiring the crushing of tomatoes before throwing to ensure that no-one (well, not too many people) got hurt. It is hard to imagine why people want to watch or even join in such nonsense, but it gains in popularity each year. At Elche, by contrast, the great annual event is the mystery-play known as the Misteri d'Eix, a rare relic of the medieval Christian past. It is a sung, liturgical drama in fifteenth century Catalan plus some Latin, while the music combines plainchant and folk tunes, all performed by local people. The festival opens with fireworks on 13 August, and on the same evening there is a dress rehearsal which is open to visitors. The play is then performed in two parts on August 14/15 for locals.

The Valencian *Falles* (Fallas in Castilian), like Buñol's *Tomatina*, has a complex history, but attracts large crowds to the city every March. The festival takes its name, meaning torches or bonfires, from the floats that are assembled for the festival, each bearing a human figure, usually satirising some aspect of the life of the region. These floats are built by various clubs from around the city, and there are also participating clubs in many of the nearby villages. After five days of partying, the floats and figures are paraded through the town and at midnight the figures, stuffed with fireworks for extra effect, are ignited. One is chosen every year to be kept intact. The *Falles* are undoubtedly of ancient origin but have tended to change their emphasis according to political circumstances. In the early years of the twentieth century, when the main political tendency in Valencia was radical and anti-clerical, church figures were often displayed on the floats, together with others from national and local government.

Despite attempts to ban the *Falles*, they survived into the Franco period, when a different approach was adopted. Overt political expression was discouraged, and religious elements inserted into the festival, unrelated to its origins but acceptable in a Catholic, corporate state. With the coming of democracy and sexual licence, critical and often obscene figures reappeared, though there is general agreement that the tone of the celebrations is socially conservative. Indeed, the *Falles* clubs, alongside the newspaper *Las Provincias* and Valencia Football Club, were major players in the domination of Valencian city politics by right-wing groups in the 1970s and 1980s such as those who fell out with Fuster, groups that on the one hand flaunt their Valencian credentials, but on the other hand are openly hostile to any attempt to link the culture and language of their homeland with that of Catalonia.

4. Popular culture in Catalonia

Popular culture in Catalonia survived Franco, but only just. Popular culture happens in the open air, in the public space, the *agora*, and the regime preferred people to live tucked away in their own flats and houses. Catalan national feeling was kept alive in many ways. The annual *festa major* continued to be celebrated in each town and village, but with a strong emphasis on the religious elements and a playing down of their civil elements and roots in pre-Christian beliefs. Members of the public, including tourists, were encouraged to watch events, rather than participating, which is a key feature of popular culture. In the Barcelona suburb of Gràcia the *festa major* shrank and nearly disappeared. The decoration of its streets had always been an essential part of the celebrations, and at one point these decorations were replaced by old shirts, satirising the old guard of Spanish fascism — the so-called *camisas viejas* (old shirts). This was sailing too close to the wind.

In Barcelona, many young people continued the long tradition of *excusionisme*, of going off to the wild mountains and woods which were seen as somehow authentic places where the spirit of Catalanism lived on, even if it could not be uttered in public. On their return on Sunday evening, a favourite gathering place was the Plaça Sant Jaume in the Old Town, where the Town Hall faces off against the Generalitat Palace, two classical façades hiding medieval Gothic interiors. The dancing of the *sardana* was in a way a façade as well. At one level just a dance, a circle of dancers performing a well-known and limited set of steps. At another level, it was highly political, because everyone knew that the dancing meant something important about the survival of Catalan

181

national feeling and the ancient language and culture of this nation. In the latter years of the Franco regime, occasional banners would be raised or leaflets distributed, and the police would step in and see off the trouble. Even during the State of Emergency in 1969 the dancing went on with (presumably) official approval, since any gathering of more than a handful of people needed official permission. There was something powerful and strong and unspoken about the *sardana*: the linked hands, always in a circle, the silent protest of a repressed people.

What happened to the *sardana* after the return of democracy shows how popular culture too has its ups and downs, its ins and outs. Whereas in the Franco days, it was easy to join a circle just by breaking a link and reforming it, the dance now feels often more of a private ritual, with organised groups coming prepared with their special shoes. They are good dancers and it is therefore much harder for a novice to join in. The key element of participation becomes less apparent, with more emphasis on spectacle and the quality of the dancing.

If there are question marks over the exclusivity of the *sardana*, this certainly does not apply to the *castellers* and this has become the fastest growing popular culture activity. The stronghold of the *castellers* has always been the area south of Barcelona especially in the towns and villages inland from Tarragona, such as Reus and Vilafranca del Penedès. But in recent years it has spread north, reaching across the French border into North Catalonia where to my knowledge there is little evidence of this ever having been popular. It has also reached Mallorca and Formentera (the small island just off the coast of Ibiza). Like the circle of the sardana dancers, human castles symbolise community strength. The activity involves people of all ages including the young children, like Tete in the film 'The Tit and the Moon', who scramble up on top of the men and women who form the lower levels of each tower. At the base of the tower is where the mass membership of the association gathers to lend their strength to the common effort, animated always by music played on traditional instruments. It is impressive, exciting, and when a castle tumbles, as sometimes happens, a risky enterprise.

In most Catalan towns, the most popular celebrations are *Carnaval* in winter and the *festa major* in summer. *Carnaval* can involve a full week of activities from the last Thursday before Lent until Ash Wednesday. The King of Fools arrives on Friday to read his sermon. There are four complete days of masked dances and street processions featuring mock battles between revellers. In Vilanova i La Geltrú on the coast south of Barcelona, the throwing of sweets, both in mock battles and more peacefully to waiting children, reflects the long nineteenth century links between the town and Cuba and its sugar industry. At least the sweets do less damage than the chunks of plaster used in the eighteenth century which were eventually banned because of the number of injuries. On Ash Wednesday the King of Fools is 'buried' in a mock funeral service; his 'will' is read, usually continuing the satirical note of the sermon. Sir James Frazer was fascinated by *Carnaval* in which he detected many echoes of pagan rites and rituals. He gives an example in *The Golden Bough* based on the report of an English traveller who witnessed wild goings-on in Lerida in 1877, a description which makes modern *Carnaval* seem quite harmless.

The summer *festa major* is the best known Catalan expression of Catalan popular culture, for the simple reason that it coincides with the peak of the tourist season. It generally includes all the features previously mentioned — *castellers*, *sardana* dancing and firework displays — but it is the processions, some held in the daytime, some at night, which are its most distinctive contribution, and which last longest in the memory of anyone fortunate enough to witness them at first hand. Each town will have its Giants and its Big-Heads, and just as the *caixers* of Menorca represent the different social classes, so the Giants will normally include a noble couple, a peasant couple and, especially in Tortosa with its long history as a centre of Muslim culture, an Arab pair. There are bands of dancers, each with their own musicians, and then there are the processional animals and birds, some realistic like the eagles and mules, some mythical like the dragons. At night the dragons will spout fire and the devils will throw firecrackers, there will be smoke and noise and confusion, and it is easy to see why any authoritarian government would have reasonable doubts about whether to permit these gloriously excessive outbursts of community spirit.

5. Popular culture as community, business and politics

Whatever reservations we might have about the *sardana*, the Moors and Christians festivals, or even very loud fireworks, there is little doubt that throughout Greater Catalonia popular culture is an important force for social cohesion and the liveliness of civil society. The *castellers* groups have been particularly successful in attracting the 'new' Catalans, immigrants from other parts of Spain and their children. In Vilanova i La Geltrú I have interviewed veteran politician Sixte Moral on a number of occasions. As first the Councillor responsible for Culture and later the town Mayor, he saw this inclusive aspect of popular culture as very important in building the new, democratic nation. He pointed to the irony that few of the Vilanova children who perform the frightening task of climbing to the summit of the castle are from Catalan-speaking families. Whereas in 1990 he was talking about the children of families with their roots within Spain, by 2001 he was referring in like manner to more recent arrivals from North Africa.

The potential of popular culture activities to bring communities together has justified local government expenditure throughout the area in support of *Carnaval*, Moors and Christians, and dance and music groups. At the same time there are other benefits, not least to the local economy, from the large amounts of money spent on fireworks, costumes, food and drink. Recent years may have been difficult from an economic point of view, with high rates of unemployment and declining real wages, but there is no sign of any willingness to cut expenditure on popular culture, either from the point of view of town council or family budgets. Festivals are also a major attraction for foreign tourists at a time when there is fierce competition from other holiday destinations. It is as if the old Franquist motto of 'Spain is Different' has returned to haunt the land. For Fraga Iribarne, Franco's Minister of Tourism, this implied different from the rest of Europe as an exotic tourist destination, but it also implies the enormous internal differences of landscape, economy and culture. Within Greater Catalonia, each land, each town, each village strives to be 'some place' rather than 'no place', a theme to which we return in the final chapter of this book. Each place strives to stamp its own distinctive mark on the cultural repertoire provided by popular culture traditions and to celebrate within the whole its own uniqueness.

Chapter 8
Catalans and Others

In Madrid newspaper editors write and play politics talking about 'We, the Spaniards ...' In Sueca, people work and harvest rice.

There's a clear trend towards escape, evasion, which is aimed at fleeing from the inimical face of immediate reality.

... the unbending resistance the literary person should put up against the devious or menacing requirements of society.

1. The tangled web of globalisation

The years since the Western European economies began to unravel following the banking crisis of 2008 have been a time of loss. The economy is not just an abstract concept. The value of bonds and shares may have fallen, but equally important — more important for those of us, the majority I believe, for whom money has always had a chimeric quality — people have lost jobs, houses, dignity; the inequalities that were already glaringly obvious in 2008 have become a running sore disfiguring the face of society; extremisms and fanaticisms of all sorts have flourished. The social welfare benefits that seemed a secure part of the social democratic settlement within the European Union have receded in the face of the new consensus that public spending must be reduced drastically, whatever the human cost.

It is hardly an age when we might expect serious commentators and politicians to engage in dispassionate debate about the future pattern of government in Spain. Needless to say, such conversations are few and far between. There is passion, there are distortions. There is a great will to wish the world were different from what it is. With every attempt by the Madrid government to close the door on discussion of the constitutional future of Catalonia, the gulf grows wider that separates public opinion in Madrid and much of the rest of Spain from public opinion on the streets of Barcelona and other Catalan towns and villages. Equally, the conviction that Madrid is opposed implacably to Catalan ambitions has narrowed debate within Catalonia itself to the false dichotomy of either/or, *Sí/No*, to independence, although as we shall see below, recent events have tended to widen out the discussion a little more. Meanwhile, the other Catalan speakers of Valencia and the islands remain completely marginal to the debate.

The crisis of living standards and livelihoods is context, but that crisis has its own context — the worldwide concentration of economic power and wealth in the hands of multinational firms and institutions. Globalisation has failed to live up to its promises of wealth and well-being for all in states which recognise international obligations, whether in relation to social welfare, human rights or the environmental damage caused by rapid industrialisation and climate change. The wealth created by global capitalism, whether in Asia or Africa, Europe or the Americas, has gouged increasingly wide fissures in society between a wealthy few and an insecure many. In the daily life of Europeans, this can mean unemployment, zero hours contracts, unofficial work outside the boundaries of proper pay and conditions, and minimum wage regulations that fail to keep pace with the cost of living. And those arrogant, wealthy elites whose obscenely bloated life-styles mock the rest of society. Additionally, the strains and stresses of life in other parts of the world drive refugees towards the shores of Europe and North America. Many die en route. Others arrive but are resented as migrant workers who (in the everyday rhetoric of casual racism promoted by the popular press and right-wing politicians) take 'our' jobs and create 'intolerable pressures' on underfunded public services such as housing and health.

This has all been going on for some time. A crucial decade was the 1980s when two contrary tendencies were afoot. On the one hand, Margaret Thatcher, UK Prime Minister, and her USA counterpart, Ronald Reagan, were applying the obscure principles of neo-liberal economic theory to the business of government. Old manufacturing industries were allowed to wither and die, new service industries were encouraged. The interests of deregulated financial services (banking, insurance) were always placed before those of productive industry. Yet on the other hand the European Union was developing precisely those social policies (the 'social market') that would define more clearly the sorts of conditions people might expect at work, and the social benefits they might expect outside of work. It is the former tendency that won out as the crisis deepened after 2008, despite the fact that it was unregulated banking structures that were everywhere responsible for the crisis.

Spain, like Greece and Portugal, which had also endured periods of right-wing military rule in the twentieth century, came late to the European Union table. Much of their industrial infrastructure fell well short of European standards. Education, social services, health services, pensions and welfare benefits — all of these needed to be developed rapidly from a very low base. Public finances were not helped by the traditional reluctance of citizens in undemocratic countries to pay taxes, a reluctance that survived the transition to democracy in Spain. (When I was working in Barcelona in the 1960s, no-one ever suggested that I should pay tax. Indeed, I was also illegal, unable to obtain a work permit, since my main employer, the university, was forbidden under a fascist law to employ foreigners. It was a strange time.) To this sorry catalogue of woe can be added the historical phenomenon of corruption, by which I mean the over-closeness of politicians and business-people, which will be dealt with later in this chapter.

None of these threatening features of the Spanish state prevented Spaniards from enjoying the 'grace of democracy', for which they had waited for forty years. They were the good times on which middle-aged writers such as Antonio Muñoz Molina looked back nostalgically as the new century headed over the cliff-tops: 'Those were the days when we thought we lived in a prosperous country in a stable world, days when we assumed the future would look like the present and things would go on getting gradually better, though perhaps at a slower rate.' (Author's translation).

There were of course warning signs, not least in the housing boom of the 1990s and 2000s. In a previous book (*Catalonia: History and Culture*, 2005) I went into some detail about national government plans to divert the waters of the River Ebro south towards the Valencian Community and Murcia, where the waters would be used to support not only agriculture and existing settlements, but also new speculative building schemes, many of them aimed at attracting migrants from northern Europe, and associated golf-courses and swimming-pools. All this in one of the driest corners of Europe. I wrote at some length about the environmental threat to the Ebro Valley, and especially the wetlands of the Ebro Delta. I wrote less about the advisability of these new housing developments, many of which now litter the countryside half-built, unloved and unwanted. I did not even mention how they were being financed, the 'sweeteners' paid to local politicians, or the astonishing failure of responsibility on the part of the banks.

The banks, of course, were doing other things than making risky loans to both developers and purchasers in the housing market. More than two years before it became common knowledge in the UK in early 2015 that the Swiss arm of HSBC was concealing the money of the rich and famous from the 'grabbing clutches' (i.e. rightful demands) of national tax authorities, Vicenç Navarro wrote an article in which he described how the Spanish media were ignoring a series of stories in the *New York Times* about such Spanish clients of HSBC as Emilio Botín, President of the Bank of Santander from 1986 until his death in 2014. Navarro claimed that Spanish citizens had enjoyed such Swiss accounts since the days of the Civil War in the 1930s. Strangely it was 2015 before this scandal, which affects citizens of a number of European countries, became widely known in the UK. The leak from an HSBC bank official suggested that Botín was just one of 569 Spanish citizens who had bene-fitted from the services of HSBC. Some unpaid tax has been collected, but no-one knows how much might yet be owing. Navarro claimed that the unpaid tax of the HSBC 569 represented three quarters of uncollected tax owed in Spain and showed that such a sum represented the figure by which Spain lagged behind the wealthiest fifteen European Union countries in terms of expenditure on social welfare.

Back in 1998, no less a figure than Prime Minister José María Aznar admitted in an interview that 'The rich do not pay taxes in Spain.' Late in 2014, it was revealed that Jordi Pujol, President of the Catalan Generalitat from 1980 to 2003, was just another Spaniard who had for many years been in the habit of squirrelling away unwanted income in overseas bank accounts. One ironical result was the quite rapid closure of the Centre d'Estudis Jordi Pujol (Study Centre), an organisation dedicated to the study of the founding father of centre-right Catalan nationalism and in particular public ethics.

When the crash came in 2008, producing what everyone refers to in both Castilian and Catalan as 'la crisis', it was not just the banks and the property devel-opers who suffered, but millions of people who suddenly found themselves unemployed, with savings and pensions worth less than expected, or with mortgages much higher than the value of their house or flat. Again, this unreality of global capitalism contrasts starkly with the reality of people's lives. As politicians and commentators talked up the prospects of the abstract 'Spanish economy', more than 21,000 concrete individuals and families lost their homes through repossession in the first six months of 2014. Those supporting a 'Yes' vote in the November 2014 Catalan 'non-referendum' laid great emphasis on tax issues, by which they meant the obvious fact that Catalonia pays more in taxes than it receives back from Madrid in grants and services. They paid less attention to the murky background of corruption, tax evasion and the self-destructive behaviour of international bankers. They had discovered one version of 'reality', but it was a very partial reality.

* * * * * * *

In a book of this sort, with an emphasis on the historical and cultural rather than the contemporary and economic, it will come as no surprise to the reader that my main concerns about globalisation centre as much on the homogenised, less differentiated way in which the world presents itself to us as on the debris of failed economies. For most people, where they live, with all its imperfections, is 'some place' rather than 'no place'. For most people place matters. It is about identity, friends, neighbours, family, lives lived in parallel, sometimes smooth, occasionally grating, the problems big and small of everyday life, resolved or accommodated. In a word, home. We all live in this somewhere of reality rather than the abstract nowhere of globalisation and the virtual reality of the Internet. It is interesting to note that after fifty years of promoting Spain — the Costas and the islands especially — as a generalised place of fun and sun, travel agencies are back again with Fraga's notion of 'Spain is Different'. Except that in this case the differences are internal: each nation, each region of Spain is keen to emphasise what is distinctive about its way of life, countryside, art and architecture, and culture.

This emphasis on the local and specific has resonance not just for tourists and visitors in search of authenticity, the lived reality of a town or village, but also for those who grow up and live there. Even those who have gone to live elsewhere as adults will make an effort to return for a *festa major*. It is not just an issue of family and friends, the people you grew up with, the language you spoke together, but of identity and emotional well-being. It is about the *soc* and *som* (I am/we are) of life, the hinge between individual, community and society. At the end of the day, such local attachments may be more important than the larger, politically charged notions of Catalan, Valencian, Balearic, Spanish or European.

The political conclusions that might be drawn from such on emphasis on local identity are extremely problematic. Many people in Greater Catalonia — most people? — live happily with the complexities of multiple identities: their place of birth, their place of residence, their sense of being at one level Catalan (or Valencian, or islanders) and at another of cultural and historical links with Spain and Europe. And for those migrants who have come to the Catalan-speaking lands from Africa, Asia or the Americas, the situation is even more complex. People do not necessarily want to be pinned down to the either/or categories of political discourse, or even the *more a than b* (or vice-versa) of social science. It is precisely these complexities which are not addressed in discussion of Catalan independence, but which become entirely to the point if the basis of discussion is Greater Catalonia and what a shared future might look like.

There is also the importance of the kind of internationalism which we saw Muñoz Molina advocating in Chapter 6, an entirely different kettle of fish from difference-ignoring globalisation. To witness, as I have witnessed, young Catalans participating whole-heartedly in solidarity work in Central America is to recognise that there is a world out there beyond the scope of this book and to which new generations might aspire. A world which erupts on our door-step every time a boatload of refugees arrives on the shores of Europe or is sunk in the process.

2. The problem of corruption

Henry Buckley, the *Daily Telegraph* correspondent in Spain in the 1930s wrote a little about Juan March, a Mallorcan businessman who had grown rich by trading with both sides in the First World War, and in the 1920s by getting his hands on the tobacco monopoly with the Moroccan territories He also owned newspapers and a bank. Jailed in 1932/1933 for dubious business activities in relation to the tobacco monopoly, he lived a life of luxury in Madrid's Modelo prison. Buckley writes: 'When I went to Palma in 1931 I went on a steamer owned by March, as I entered Palma harbour, I saw a petrol refinery, it belonged to March; I saw a fertilizer factory, it belonged to March; I changed my money at a March bank and even when I paid a visit to the local Casa del Pueblo, trade union headquarters, I was told that it "was given us by Sr. March".'

Such links between business and politicians go back a long way. Much of the decline of Catalonia and Valencia after 1492 was not just about the reorientation of Spain away from the Mediterranean and towards the Atlantic and the Americas. It was a specific decision by the Spanish crown to give Seville a monopoly on trade with the colonies which turned the dynamic Mediterranean ports of Barcelona, Valencia and Alicante into backwaters. This monopoly lasted for 200 years, a period during which gold and silver from South America was used not to develop Spain itself, but to finance Hapsburg adventures elsewhere in Europe.

There was also the issue of the church and its power, including vast estates handed over to the church as the

Christian kingdoms expanded southwards in the late Middle Ages. Historic monastic sites in Catalonia such as Santes Creus and Poblet are just small reminders of this period. From the mid-eighteenth century, the state attempted to curb the power of the church, first by expelling the Jesuits and then in the 1830s by expropriating church lands. Juan Álvarez Mendizábal returned from exile in England in 1835 to become Minister of Finance in a Liberal government. He had become convinced of the virtues of the free market, as laid down by Adam Smith, and clearly also knew about King Henry VIII and the economic benefits of the dissolution of the English monasteries. A law was passed declaring that most church land was now state land. It could now be sold at auction, thus benefiting state coffers but also bringing a potential new dynamism to the economy. Soon four-fifths of church land in Barcelona had been sold off. Three quarters of the church lands in Catalonia in both town and country were sold between 1837 and 1845, largely to the benefit of the urban middle classes. Elsewhere in Spain, it was often the nobility who profited from the sale of church land, but there is clear evidence that in Valencia and Alicante provinces, smaller tenant farmers were able to get their hands on new land, and the success of nineteenth century agriculture in the Valencian Community may be related to this.

Juan March set the tone for business-politics relations into the twentieth century. According to Paul Preston's biography of Franco, it was a blank cheque from March which enabled the military plotters in July 1936 to hire a Dragon Rapide at Croydon Airport which eventually transported Franco from the Canary Islands to Spanish possessions in Morocco. The example of the Muñoz brothers (Álvaro and Julio) will give a flavour of the period. In Barcelona, they made very large amounts of money from the black market, subsequently invested in the purchase of a major slice of the Catalan textile industry (1944) and large property holdings in the city. "Después de

Dios, los hermanos Muñoz" (God first, the Muñoz brothers next) went the popular saying. Julio married into a Spanish banking empire, and his later acquisitions included a Swiss bank. No doubt this facilitated his residence in Switzerland in the 1980s as the net closed around him. There is also the extraordinary story of his acquisition of public art treasures which he much later donated back (well, most of them) to the city of Barcelona. All of the activities of the brothers were smoothed along by his supporters in the Franco regime at both local and national level. It was the closeness and secretiveness of the regime that facilitated corruption, and in its later stages, such dubious business activities were carried forward into an era of relative economic expansion with the arrival in Franco's immediate circle of the young tigers of the secretive Catholic organisation Opus Dei (the Work of God). In imitation of the words of the Latin mass, their detractors would recite: "Opus Dei, qui tollis pecunia mundi, dona nobis partem." (Opus Dei, which taketh away the cash of the world, grant us a share).

Corruption, the too close conjoining of business and politics, is not new in Spain. The surprise is that it survived the 1970s transition to democracy. Secrecy was not just the prerogative of the Right. Felipe González was Prime Minister from 1982–1996 and brought with him a number of leading members of the PSOE (Socialist Party) whose relations had been formed in Seville in the last years of the Franco regime, when political parties were still illegal. There is no doubt that these close and secretive clandestine methods of working continued into the period of PSOE rule and gave rise both to scandals and, what is as bad for a democracy, rumours of scandals, as the Spanish economy was turned upside down to prepare Spain for European Union membership. Alfonso Guerra, a close ally of González and deputy Prime Minister from 1982–1991 was forced to resign when it became public that his brother Juan was occupying public buildings in Seville without an explicit government function. Public contracts were awarded to firms close to the PSOE leadership, while membership of the party was claimed to enhance one's job prospects in the public sector.

Unfortunately, the Popular Party, the main beneficiary of corruption claims against PSOE, proved as adept as the socialists at using similar methods when it was their turn to govern, especially as the property bubble inflated at the beginning of the new century. In part, it was a question of securing planning rights for new developments, but also an issue of which firms won contracts for the grandiose public building schemes which began to be such a feature of towns large and small in Spain. The Catalan-speaking world had its fair share of scandals. Those in Valencia were mentioned in chapter 4. On the little island of Formentera, the Popular Party went a little further, by adding to the electoral register the names of 74 voters who had left the island years earlier to emigrate to Latin America. Needless to say, they all 'voted' for PP, and since this particular scandal became public, the Formenterencs have voted consistently for other parties.

The one regime which appeared to have escaped this murky world of favours, backhanders and outright lawbreaking was the Catalan autonomous government. Yet precisely at a period when the issue of Catalan independence was moving to centre stage in the second half of 2014, it was revealed that Jordi Pujol, President of the Generalitat from 1980–2003, had been hoarding away profits from his family pharmaceutical company in overseas bank accounts to avoid paying tax in Spain. Other members of the family are implicated, in particular his politically active son Jordi who has been accused of accepting illegal commissions on contracts awarded by the Generalitat. There is little doubt that this scandal has had a direct impact on the falling away of support for the CiU alliance, and the difficulties that President Mas has had in showing real leadership in the constitutional debate.

In so many ways, the issue of how to move politics onto a more honest, open footing seems as important as the issue of Catalan independence or of the relations between the Catalan-speaking lands. For the anti-nationalist novelist Juan Marsé, a lover of the complex and beautiful city of Barcelona, the issue is quite clear. In a 2014 interview with Elena Hevia in *El Periódico*, he put it very bluntly indeed: 'I am not a nationalist, in the first place because I don't share that sentimental identification that so many people feel just because they were born either here or there, and in second place because I have no reason to think that in an independent Catalonia, those who govern, to judge by the ones we have now, the ones who are proposing this change, will be less corrupt, less inept and less stupid than their Spanish counterparts, that's to say, I know that both lots are going to fuck me up because that's what they do. I don't trust those people. At the moment, it's all the same whether I'm Spanish or Catalan, since neither of the two options excites me.' Harsh words, but sometimes a nation (Spain? Catalonia?) needs to hear voices like that.

3. 2015: a year of elections

For Catalonia, 2015 was the year of crucial regional elections which were to set a path either towards or away from independence. Yet in the middle of all the excitement, posturing and manoeuvring for the Catalan elections in September, a further set of elections intervened in May. These involved Barcelona City Council, as well as the regional governments of Valencia and the Balearic Islands. In Barcelona independence was far from the only show in town, and in a shock result the municipal election was won by Ada Colau at the head of a citizens' group called Barcelona en Comú (Barcelona in Common), an ally of the social activists' party Podemos. From 2009–2014 the new Mayor had achieved fame — her opponents would say notoriety — leading PAH, a direct action and lobbying organisation working with people threatened by eviction for non-payment of mortgages. Barcelona en Comú received only one-fifth of the votes, but as leader of the largest council group she became Mayor with the support of socialist (PSC) and republican (ERC) councillors. One of her first symbolic acts was the removal of a bust of the recently abdicated King Juan Carlos from Barcelona Town Hall. She is also the author with Adrià Alemany of an acclaimed book *Vidas Hipotecadas* (the English version *Mortgaged Lives* is available as a free Internet download). She represents, in a very real way, the Barcelona of poverty and austerity that the tourists do not see.

While Ada Colau was winning her historic victory in Barcelona, equally exciting changes were taking place in the political make-up of the Valencian Community and Balearic Islands, both previously ruled by the conservative party PP. In both sets of regional elections, PP emerged as the largest party, but political control passed to the socialists (PSOE) and their allies. In the island assembly these allies were Podemos and the left nationalists of Més per Mallorca and Més per Menorca. In the Valencian Community, the socialists rely for support on Podemos and Compromís (in both Castilian and Catalan this means commitment rather than compromise). Compromís is an alliance of a number of left-wing, nationalist and green parties and is now an important political force throughout the community, especially on issues of language use and the environment. In both regions, the so-called tri-lingual educational reforms are likely to be scrapped, while the Balearic government is once more considering the desirability of a tourist tax to be used for environmental protection.

* * * * * * *

We now know that over one and a half million Catalans — those who voted Yes-Yes in the November 2014 consultation — are in favour of independence. We know there is a smaller number — the less than half a million who voted No-No — who are bitterly opposed. We know far less about those who chose not to vote, although opinion polls have consistently suggested about 45% in favour of independence, a figure remarkably similar to the Yes vote in the 2014 Scottish referendum. However, 'consistent' hardly describes the opinion polling, since this figure is fifteen points down from the 60% in favour at one point in 2014. It appeared that the bubble of independence support has been pricked, but it is more difficult to determine exactly who was wielding the pin. The ball is back firmly in the court of the politicians and they have failed since the November 2014 vote to give any kind of clear lead. Coalitions are crumbling. CiU broke up into its two constituent parts, with the larger liberal half, Convergència Democràtica de Catalunya (CDC), supporting independence and the Christian Democrat UDC wing opposing. Following the November 2014 consultation, the ruling CiU-ERC coalition was expected to call early elections as a substitute for a referendum. Yet even after the CiU break-up, CDC and ERC took a very long time to agree on a common list of candidates, much to the frustration of the grassroots Catalanist movements such as the Catalan National Assembly (ANC) and Òmnium Cultural. Eventually President Mas did call for an election on 27 September 2015, scarcely the snap election that had been expected. A common list of candidates was agreed, to be presented to the electorate with leaders of the civil society Catalanist movements heading the list, and Mas as presidential candidate. The name chosen was Junts pel Sí (Together for Yes).

In working towards the Catalan elections of 27 September 2015, Mas also had the support of the radical independentists of CUP (Popular Unity), although they refused to join the Junts pel Sí coalition, being convinced neither by the Road Map laid out towards a declaration of independence 'within 18 months' or by Mas as a leader. Activity in the 'No' camp continued in a variety of ways with no clear consensus. The PP, scarcely helped by the increasingly hostile tone of the Madrid government and mired by charges of corruption in both national government and the regional governments it controlled, has proved an ineffective force compared to Ciutadans (Citizens). Originally set up to oppose independence in Catalonia, this has become a national Spanish party as Ciudadanos, representing a younger and more progressive looking conservatism, untainted by corruption and lingering memories of the Franco regime. It has placed more stress on social issues such as the possible impact of independence on public sector pensions in Catalonia.

The citizen-based party, Podemos, has avoided carefully pronouncing in favour of or against independence. At the same time, they are the one party that is clearly committed at a Spanish level to some form of constitutional review. Their leader, Pablo Iglesias, received a warm welcome in Barcelona just before Christmas 2014. Without committing himself to particular policies, especially an independence referendum, he showed clear support for the 'right to decide' which must have pleased Catalans while begging the question of exactly what they might decide. Given the intransigence of the traditional parties, his offer to 'extend bridges rather than build walls' must have been music to Catalan ears. With the Spanish general election due to take place shortly after the Catalan elections of September 2015, his speech did hold out some hope of an unblocking of the log-jam of debate about Catalonia's future. And the singing of Lluís Llach's 1968 anti-Franco anthem 'L'Estaca' ('The Stake') was a reminder that the future of Catalonia is just one piece in the jigsaw of Spain's still youthful democracy: 'If I pull it hard this way/And you pull it hard that way/Then pull, pull, pull it down/And we can all be free'.

The other two traditional Spanish parties (socialist and conservative) remain opposed to independence. The socialists favour a more federalist structure for Spain, while the Popular Party simply says 'No'. Like Iglesias, Prime

Minister Mariano Rajoy visited Barcelona in the aftermath of the November 2014 consultation, but with a rather different agenda in mind. He described the vote as a resounding failure, and denounced the 'international propaganda operation' mounted by the Catalan government. He also emphasised that two thirds of Catalans had not voted, which was an odd claim to make since it was Popular Party inclined members of the Constitutional Court who had declared the planned referendum illegal. Rajoy has exploited successfully a deep vein of anti-Catalan sentiment in Spain, but in doing so he has offered Catalans little incentive to remain part of Spain, at least on the existing terms. His increasingly shrill demonization of the Catalans seemed like a desperate attempt to cling on to power nationally.

The issue of who won the Catalan elections is an interesting one. Junts pel Sí and their Popular Unity allies achieved a majority of seats in the Generalitat, but only 48% of the votes cast. The difference is due to the weighting of votes in the four Catalan provinces to prevent the voice of the more rural areas being drowned out by urban Barcelona. Thus Mas had a potential parliamentary majority would will allow him to declare independence 'within 18 months' but not the kind of popular mandate which might give his independence movement international legitimacy. The one clear outcome of the election was that it produced a majority for parties supporting Catalonia's right to decide, including Podemos and its anti-austerity allies. The Madrid government remained committed to opposing independence by all legal means possible, yet only had two months to run.

The final election of the year was the Spanish General Election on 20 December 2015. For months the opinion polls had remained static, with the conservative PP leading from the socialist PSOE, but both parties showing considerable falls in support compared with previous elections. The two-party system that had dominated Spain for so long was dead, and the election results buried it.

Instead, four parties emerged with substantial levels of support – in order of popularity: PP – 123 seats, PSOE – 90 seats, Podemos – 69 seats, and Ciudadanos – 40 seats. 176 seats is the figure needed for a majority. Intriguingly, Podemos, supported by Barcelona's new Mayor, had gathered the largest number of votes in Catalonia, after finally declaring support for a Catalan referendum. Yet there was no obvious coalition capable of forming a government. The solution that had been achieved in Valencia and the Balearics, with smaller parties gathering around PSOE was a difficult option because of PSOE's preference for constitutional reform over a Catalan referendum. A German-style 'grand coalition' of conservatives and socialists, plus Ciudadanos, looked unlikely because of traditional hostilities between the two parties. By mid-January 2016, voices were being raised in PP in support of very modest constitutional reform, scarcely enough to satisfy the socialists let alone the Catalan supporters of independence. A minority PP government based on abstentions in crucial votes by PSOE and Ciudadanos seemed one possible way forward.

At the time that this book went to press, it seemed that whatever government is cobbled together in Madrid would be weak and unlikely to last for long. It will not be a good basis from which to discuss either Catalan independence or a possible new constitutional settlement within Spain. One further development in Catalonia is worth noting. The Popular Unity (CUP) members of the Catalan Parliament refused on several occasions to endorse Artur Mas as President because of his long association with the corrupt Jordi Pujol. After nearly four months of argument and debate (the election had taken place in September 2015) and just as fresh elections seemed inevitable, Mas gave way to Carles Puigdemont, ex-Mayor of the CDC stronghold of Gerona, as presidential candidate. President Puigdemont was then endorsed by parliament in January 2016. One way forward for both Spain and Catalonia is a generational renewal of their leaders.

4. Greater Catalonia — where is the political project?

Spain, at least, is a political project, albeit a failing one. Catalonia, it seems, has just become one as a result of the 2015 Catalan elections, the Road Map towards independence. Whether it will reach that goal, the reader of this book in coming years will be better placed to judge than its author. The socialist and conservative parties which have dominated Spanish politics for the past 30 years have a shared view of the essential unity of the Spanish state, and its place within Europe (the European Union) and in the world (the United Nations) as a nation among nations. In both political projects — Spain and Catalonia — there are endemic weaknesses such as corruption and rumours of corruption which weaken the moral force and direction of movement. These in turn have given rise to a much more pluralist democracy in which new parties appear, often closely linked to social movements opposing corruption and/or austerity. The Spanish and Catalan political projects will persist but may adopt different forms in the future,

But in the case of Greater Catalonia and the historic ties between the Catalan-speaking lands, there is nothing on the blue Mediterranean horizon that even begins to resemble a political project. Maybe there are small numbers of people in Valencia, Alicante, Palma, even Perpignan, who still retain faith in the 'cause' of Greater Catalonia, but there is little sense of how that might be achieved. While nationalists on the islands and in the Valencian Community performed well in the 2015 regional elections, they have achieved success at least in part by distancing themselves from the historical notion of the *Països Catalans*. In many ways, as the possibility of an independent Catalonia draws closer, the cause of Great Catalonia seems farther away than ever. Even cultural links seems weaker than ten or twenty years ago. The joint Catalonia — Balearic Islands Ramon Llull

Institute was established in 2002, its aim to promote Catalan language and culture. In 2012, the Balearic Islands government decided to cease supporting it, although following the 2015 elections, discussions opened paving the way for the islands to rejoin the institute. The Valencian Community has never been a member. During the early years of the transition to democracy, there was considerable twin town activity between the Valencian Community and Catalonia, but this ceased some years ago.

The suggestion that some members of ERC want a clause on Greater Catalonia in a 'Catalan' constitution does nothing to calm relations between Catalans and their neighbours. It is not just Madrid-orientated members of the Popular Party in Valencia and Palma who deride the notion of being ruled from Barcelona, and raise this in defence of their own sense of a primary Spanish identity. Many of those who value their use of Catalan (as Valencian, Mallorcan and so on) in daily life, who have that shared sense of a historical Catalan identity, shudder at the thought of ever being part of a Catalan state. For them, national identity begins at home, as Valencians, Mallorcans or Menorcans. It as if someone were to suggest that Irish, Scots, Welsh and Cornish should join forces in a political union simply because of common Celtic roots.

And yet in some ways, the Celtic comparison may suggest a way forward. Any summer visitor to Cornwall will notice the frequency with which Cornish communities are twinned with those in Brittany. The annual Inter-Celtic Festival at Lorient in Brittany attracts musicians and performers from all the Celtic nations, including contingents from Galicia and Asturias in Spain, where the ancient Celtic roots have sprouted healthy green shoots in recent years. Such a cultural expression of Greater Catalonia does not preclude a political project but is likely to garner much greater support in the medium term. At the moment, the politics — Spain, Catalonia — are putting up barriers rather than building bridges.

Catalonia and Valencia, Roussillon and the Balearic Islands too, have both common interests and separate interests. This has been the case through history. As Joan Mira has written, 'Catalonia and Valencia are always two territories or countries; part of the same Crown and subjects of the same King of Aragon, but not just one state; and so the Valencian insistence on an autonomous political status does not respond to mere chance, but to a solid, substantial social reality.' (Author's translation; Mira's emphasis). So whether it is a matter of economic development or political reality, there is some potential in a looser alignment between the Catalan-speaking lands than has been suggested in previous thinking about Greater Catalonia.

A minor breakthrough in recent years has been the concept of a Catalan Commonwealth. Significantly it has come from a geographer rather than an expert on language and culture. If the idea of a British Commonwealth no longer arouses great interest in modern Britain, it has recently been used in this rather unlikely context to describe the common interests of Valencia and Catalonia. Josep Vicent Boira (*La Commonwealth Catalanovalenciana*, 2009) is an economic geographer rather than a political thinker, and emphasises the common economic interests of these two nations. He reminds both Catalans and Valencians that good economic relations have always existed, and that the notion of an economic corridor in an age of free trade is entirely compatible with the mud-slinging that the Valencian and Catalan parliaments engage in from time to time. Presumably such a corridor might also be extended to include the south of France and the Balearic Islands. Boira points out that anti-Catalanism may be a good political vote-catcher in Valencia but makes little business sense. From a Catalan point of view, he urges Catalonia to establish better relations with its immediate neighbours as part of a strategy of projecting itself on a European and international stage. The mid-term aim of both Valencians and Catalans should be to 'form a strong economic, social and intellectual region in this part of the Mediterranean.'

Boira acknowledges political tensions, but asserted in an interview in 2014 that 'our societies are much more than just one government or another: they include universities, the media, civil society, not to mention the citizens who, despite everything, still fill the trains and the motorways of the Mediterranean axis.' In a provocative review in *La Vanguardia* in 2010, Enric Juliana described Boira's idea as a new 'Trojan Horse', a way of breaking the impasse created by bad feeling in both Catalonia and Valencia about their neighbours, and the fading star of illusions about Greater Catalonia. Juliana picks up too on the curious (to British ears) references to the British Commonwealth. For Juliana is has the 'British attraction of practical common sense', the same pragmatic approach that was so appealing to 'Catalans and Valencians of the industrial era'. Presumably for a Valencian, the term does not carry the baggage of racism, imperial ambition and royalist bowing and scraping it might have here in Britain.

Ideas have a way of dodging in and out of sight, like the sun disappearing behind the moon at a solar eclipse. The idea of a Catalan-Valencian Commonwealth, extended to embrace the people of Roussillon and the Balearic Islands, is most certainly not on everybody's lips at a time (2015) when the possibility of Catalan independence dominates public debate. Yet it has a number of attractions. Not only is it eminently practical (though I doubt if the British have a monopoly on pragmatism) but it also brings into play the essential Mediterranean nature of Catalan history — those highways across the sea that have been so influential since prehistoric (I prefer pre-literate) times. Highways that have carried new trade goods and new technologies, new ideas and beliefs, from one end of the inland ocean to the other.

5. Spain and Catalonia: government and civil society

Sagest of women, even of widows, she
  Resolved that Juan should be quite a paragon,
And worthy of the noblest pedigree:
  (His sire was of Castile, his dam from Arragon).
(Byron, Don Juan, Canto I)

It is only peoples who lack deep unity who will put such fatal emphasis upon it and who will corrupt the idea of unity and make it uniformity
(V.S. Pritchett, The Spanish Temper, 1954)

In this final chapter, I have felt it necessary to address the issue of Spain, because it is now clear that it is the weakness of the Spanish state that is driving the push for independence in Catalonia, and at the same time poisoning good relations between the peoples of Greater Catalonia. There is no deep-rooted conspiracy by the Catalans to move from autonomous region to independent state, in order to express that clear sense they have of being a nation. If there has been a conspiracy, then surely it has gone in the opposite direction as Madrid has pushed Catalonia away.

In particular the Spanish Popular Party has used its majority supporters in the Constitutional Court to claw back the more extensive autonomous powers negotiated with Madrid by the Generalitat and approved overwhelmingly by the Catalans in a referendum. In the process, they have not only politicised a tribunal intended to be above politics, but also exposed as a sham the present autonomous regime in Spain, which attempts to equate the historical claims to nationhood of Basques and Catalans with the much looser regional feelings of areas such as La Rioja. As I argued in chapter 1 from the work of Muñoz Molina, it is an unwieldy, expensive and fragmented system of government.

The argument about Catalan independence is also an argument about whether it is possible to 'save Spain' from itself. A hefty slice of the problem is the very low level of political debate in Spain. Just to give one small example. In early 2015, Spain's Foreign Secretary, José Manuel García Margallo claimed that the Podemos citizens' party was not only receiving money from Venezuela "but also from Russia", even suggesting "there are unconfirmed rumours [they are receiving money] from Iran as well". He did not offer any more details but said Podemos should be as transparent as the party demands others be, "when the funds come from foreign powers that could condition national politics". (From *The Spain Report*, March 2015). The level of political debate is low in most countries, given the insatiable search by 24-hour news media for gossip, rumour, innuendo, anything in fact but hard news and rigorous analysis. But for a senior politician to make such claims hiding behind 'unconfirmed rumours' is an extraordinary way to conduct discussion. In the final days of the 2015 Catalan election campaign, the Spanish Prime Minister asserted that Catalans would lose their Spanish nationality, despite a clause in the Spanish constitution which safeguards nationality for Spaniards living in 'a foreign country.' It was a statement unworthy of a democratic politician.

Madrid politicians have poured scorn and derision over their Barcelona counterparts in recent years, a splendid technique to avoid the intricacies of argument. They might, for example have reserved rather more of their criticism for the dubious logic of some of the arguments of the Catalan independentists. For example, the fiscal deficit argument that claims (correctly) that more money is raised in Catalonia through taxation than is returned by central government in grants and services. This is of course exactly the argument used by those opposed to the European Union when they see the richer nations of the north and west subsidising the poorer nations of the south and east. It is also the argument within nations of those who propose tax cuts for the wealthy as a way of reversing the historic trend within democracies for tax revenue to flow from the wealthy to the poor, a reversal which is now well established in the UK.

A second argument they might have questioned is that of the *'dret de decidir'* (right to decide) claimed by the Catalan people. The Madrid politicians of both Left and Right have focused on the way that a vote on independence is expressly prohibited by the Spanish Constitution, rather less on what exactly it is that the Catalans want to have the right to decide. Kathryn Crameri's 2014 book *Goodbye Spain? The question of independence for Catalonia* has revived again the use by Jaume Vicens i Vives (in *Notícia de Catalunya*, 1950) of the metaphor of the Minotaur as the abstract embodiment of power. In English, we might say more humbly that Catalonia has failed consistently to grasp the nettle of power. Crameri writes that 'a fundamental question about the recent rise in support for independence is the extent to which people really have now accepted the idea of a Catalan state, as opposed simply to taking pro-independence positions in opposition to the Spanish state. In other words, does the rhetoric of the 'right to decide' actually conceal the same lack of commitment to the idea of the state that Vicens Vives identified as a constant characteristic of the Catalan nation?'

Whereas the policies of ERC would seem to suggest a critique of European Union austerity programmes, rooted in turn in the policies of the International Monetary Fund, the other recent convert to independence, CDC, would appear to support the same neo-liberal economic policies as the conservative Spanish government. There has also been little discussion of whether an independent Catalonia would be a monarchy (support for which has declined throughout Spain) or a republic. There are many international commitments which appear to constrain the independence that Catalonia might achieve, chief among them the European Union, international trade agreements, multinational companies and banks, and NATO. It is not at all clear what Catalan independence would be like in practice, whether Catalan politicians would pull against the chains that would continue to bind them, or accept them as part of the way of the world.

I concluded a previous book on Catalonia (*Catalonia: History and Culture*, 2004, revised edition 2009) by quoting Lluís Llach's 1975 song '*Viatge a Itaca*' (Journey to Ithaca) in which he used the well-known poem by C.P. Cavafy to emphasise the importance of Odysseus' quest for Ithaca rather than his arrival home. Yet more recently, it is as if Ithaca has become the goal of independence, rather than the goal of democracy as a way to transform the world. The words Llach added to Cavafy remain very relevant, concluding: 'And when you think you have arrived, have the courage to keep travelling'; in search of such holy grails as social justice. Exactly what the Catalans might do with independence is still a well-kept secret. The future, like the past, remains an unknown country. What follows is just one Utopian suggestion.

* * * * * * *

Just as Catalonia, Valencia and the Balearic Islands will eventually have to sink their differences and behave again like the good neighbours they have usually been, the same applies to wider relations in the Mediterranean world. In 2014, over 3,000 people died in a vain effort to migrate from the troubled world of the Maghreb and the Middle East to Europe. A similar total is likely in 2015, and the subject of migration into Europe is now high on the agenda of all European governments. At last, serious conversations have started about how to balance the push factors (poverty, war, civil unrest) and the pull factors (the open labour market and internal borders of the European Union). Like the Catalan-Valencian Commonwealth idea, it may seem a curious moment in history to float this particular idea. Yet bringing stability and sustainable development to North Africa, and peace and reconciliation to the Middle East are the two necessary steps to prevent the current horrors of Mediterranean life. The Spanish (I include here Catalans, Valencians and islanders) have always had a special relationship with the southern shores of the Mediterranean and are in a unique position to act as midwife in the birth of more equal relations between its two shores. Respect for difference, yes, but acceptance of the present pattern of gross inequalities, no.

Once again, Lluís Llach is the man who sums up the potential unity of this very divided and confused Mediterranean world. In 'Pont de Mar Blava' (A Bridge of Blue Sea) he sets a poem by an older Catalan poet, Miquel Martí i Pol, which deals with past and present, with the many shores of the Mediterranean from Catalonia to Lebanon, with personal and public memory, all infused with that interior sublimated anger that the two artists share. Finally, then, it comes down to this –

> Un pont de mar blava per sentir-nos frec a frec,
> un pont que agermani pells i vides
> diferents,
> diferents.

> *(A bridge of blue sea to feel close to one another, / A bridge that brings together skins and lives / Different, / Different.)*

Victor Alba, a veteran of the Spanish War of 1936-39 spent six years in Franco's prisons before eventually creating a new life for himself as a writer and North American university professor. He finished his 1975 book *Catalonia: a Profile* with the hope that being a Catalan would become a normal state of affairs one day rather than an issue that has to be worried over. He wrote: 'He (sic) will be able to be himself as well as an integral part of Spain and Europe. He will be able to enjoy his natural identity instead of defending it. He will have passed from the winter quarters of nationalism into the free air of a nation in a group of nations. On that day there no longer will be any Catalan problem, and those who write about Catalonia will no longer have to walk a tightrope between objectivity and partisanship. *How I envy them*!' (Alba's

emphasis) Forty years later the matter remains unre-
solved. The tightrope remains too. And of course it is also
possible that the Catalans may decide that, like the
Valencians and Mallorcans, the Menorcans and Ibizans,
the people of Roussillon and Formentera, they are happy
to be a people among peoples rather than a nation among
nations.

The Right Word

English	French/Spanish	Catalan/Valencian	Use in book
France			
Perpignan	Perpignan	Perpinyà	Perpignan
Roussillon	Roussillon	Catalunya Nord	North Catalonia
Islands			
Balearic Islands	Islas Baleares	Illes Balears	Balearic Islands
Minorca	Menorca	Menorca	Menorca
Majorca	Mallorca	Mallorca	Mallorca
Ibiza	Ibiza	Eivissa	Ibiza
Autonomous Regions			
Catalonia	Cataluña	Catalunya	Catalonia
Valencia	Valencia	Comunitat Valènciana	Valencia or Valencian Community
Provinces and provincial capitals			
Gerona	Gerona	Girona	Gerona
Lerida	Lérida	Lleida	Lerida
Barcelona	Barcelona	Barcelona	Barcelona
Castellon	Castellón de la Plana	Castelló de la Plana	Castellon
Valencia	Valencia	València	Valencia or Valencia City
Alicante	Alicante	Alacant	Alicante
Other towns and cities in Greater Catalonia			
Alcoy	Alcoy	Alcoi	Alcoy
Denia	Denia	Dénia	Denia
Elche	Elche	Eix	Elche
Figueres	Figueras	Figueres	Figueres
Mahon	Mahón	Maó	Mahon
Peniscola	Peñíscola	Peníscola	Peniscola
Xativa	Játiva	Xátiva	Xativa
Other Spanish cities			
Cadiz	Cádiz	Cadis	Cadiz
Cordoba	Córdoba	Còrdova	Cordoba
Seville	Sevilla	Sevilla	Seville
Saragossa	Zaragoza	Saragossa	Saragossa